Between *the* Idea *and the* Reality

Praise for *Between the Idea & the Reality*

This book is a masterclass in educational leadership. Norm Hunter assembles an eclectic range of sources to augment his practical wisdom as a successful founder and long-term leader of a vibrant school community. It's a must-have resource for any team or individual looking to build a principled mental model of leadership that actually works.

Professor Erica McWilliam AM, ACEL fellow

Every leader needs a mentor and I have found one in Norm Hunter who has nurtured my leadership for the past 12 years. This book is filled with the wisdom gained over many years of school leadership and is a must-read for principals and school leaders. The materials and questions contained within the pages will guide them in their roles and most importantly help them become a mentor for others.

Mark Cridland, Principal

Leadership in schools – and in life – is complex and messy. This book doesn't shy away from that, but nor does it patronise with formulaic tools or "quick fixes". Skilfully blending timeless wisdom, fresh insights, and practical examples, Norm Hunter invites us to consider the humanity of leadership, the importance of careful decision-making, and the value of working collectively. Reading it feels like being mentored by an exceptional teacher, leader, and guide. It's practical and it's inspirational: a book to sustain leaders; a book to savour and to share.

Karen Fox, Educator, Learner, Facilitator

This book represents no less than a career of professional service in drawing people out and leading them on, synthesised without simplicity into an utterly engaging and entirely practical tale about the deeply complex work of the leadership of young people and adults in schools. It is at once informative and vividly illuminating to both current and aspiring educators who may wish to see more clearly that their journey is not along a road never taken; that nuance truly matters; and that they have a hope for their own becoming.

Alexander Mason, Curriculum Leader, ACEL fellow

This is a must-read for any educational leader or anyone aspiring to that position. The author poses questions which are wonderfully thought provoking, and I just wish that this book had been available to me when I was a high school principal. It is written in an informative and interesting way, and I loved the apt quotations throughout the book.

Yvonne Hill OAM

I just love it. Its huge strength is its insight – it is deceptively simple yet is so complex. The narrative is compelling and introduces the reader to deep thought. It contextualises so many complex themes in the context of academic theory and English literature, introduces a lifetime of thought, and breathes life into the academic literature both old and new. It's a beautifully contextual narrative. I hope it is used widely for both educational leadership courses at universities and for thought provocation in schools.

Dr Bruce Addison, Deputy Principal

In this book Norm Hunter challenges the reader to ponder educational issues and questions that rarely get discussed in the leadership literature but are critically relevant to all school communities. It is a distillation of wisdom, accrued over many years of experience as a principal of a metropolitan co-educational school, an educational networker, and a lover of literature; *Between the Idea and Reality* takes us to the human core of effective educational leadership. The result is an engaging read, rewarded with practical gems for all leaders to take back into their schools.

Jacqui Zervos, Deputy Principal

His great skill is the ability to synthesise the wisdom and messages of credible education researchers and practitioners and cleverly mould them into uncomplicated, almost counter-intuitive, lessons for leaders. I found the book quietly reassuring and encouraging for those of us who fear we are losing control of the educational agenda to ideology, politics, and bureaucracy, and a few others. The messages fit beautifully within the Catholic context, and I will definitely be adding this to our professional learning strategy resources.

Dr Pat Coughlan, Executive Director, Catholic Education

Between *the* Idea *and the* Reality

Decision-Making for the Thinking Educational Leader

Norman Hunter

Published in 2024 by Amba Press, Melbourne, Australia

www.ambapress.com.au

© Norman Hunter 2024

All rights reserved. No part of this book may be reproduced or transmitted in any form or by any means, electronic or mechanical, including photocopying, recording or by any information storage and retrieval system, without prior permission in writing from the publisher.

Cover design: Tess McCabe
Internal design: Amba Press
Editor: Andrew Campbell

ISBN: 9781923215269 (pbk)
ISBN: 9781923215276 (ebk)

A catalogue record for this book is available from the National Library of Australia.

To Rae, my soul-mate and best friend,
without whom I'd be a lesser person.

I owe much to Emeritus Professor Frank Crowther,
who opened a world of research to me and encouraged
my thinking in ways no-one had done before.

"Between the idea
And the reality ...
Falls the shadow."

– T. S. Eliot

"Thoughts are but dreams till their effects be tried."

– William Shakespeare

"Decisions are made by people. People are fallible; at best their works do not last long. Even the best decision has a high probability of being wrong. Even the most effective one eventually becomes obsolete."

– Peter Drucker

Contents

Foreword	Emeritus Professor Frank Crowther	xi
About the author		xv
Acknowledgements		xvii
Prologue		1
Chapter 1	A marijuana leaf and an octopus	5
Chapter 2	The age of ambiguity	9
Chapter 3	A long and winding road	17
Chapter 4	Going back ... to go forward	20
Chapter 5	Just what the truth is ...	27
Chapter 6	The way it is	34
Chapter 7	A roadmap or a compass?	42
Chapter 8	The management of meaning	47
Chapter 9	Competing principles	60
Chapter 10	Who won the race?	66
Chapter 11	What we can't see	71
Chapter 12	Culture and structure	76
Chapter 13	A leadership framework	81
Chapter 14	Culture (1): The art of the Covenant	90
Chapter 15	Culture (2): Walking in two worlds	94
Chapter 16	Culture (3): The power of trust	104
Chapter 17	Culture (4): The power of hope	115

Chapter 18	Intuition (1)	129
Chapter 19	Intuition (2)	140
Chapter 20	Intuition (3)	145
Chapter 21	Conflict avoidance, bias and noise	150
Chapter 22	To know the place for the first time	161
Chapter 23	The power of metaphor	166
Chapter 24	The power of story	180
Chapter 25	Where it all leads	188

Afterword	190
References	192

Foreword

Emeritus Professor Frank Crowther

This book by Norm Hunter transcends time and space. It answers questions that have dogged educational administration throughout its history and it has application wherever educational administration is practised. Educational leaders who aspire to enriching their "big picture" understanding of their daily practice will find the chapters that follow immensely valuable.

When educational administration as a field of professional practice first saw the light of day (at a select group of American universities, most notably Chicago and Ohio), decision-making was a clear and unmistakable focus. Effective decision-making on the part of leaders – including airline pilots, bishops, business executives and school principals – was seen as the essential key to bringing tradition and change into harmonious integration. For three decades, from about 1950 to the 1980s, processes of decision-making retained that central place as educational administration became an accepted field of study and spread its wings globally, including in Australia.

Wonderful concepts emerged during these fertile decades. Perhaps most notably, Herbert Simon's ground-breaking "general theory of administration" in 1950 proclaimed that any such theory "must include principles of organisation that will ensure correct decision-making". Then, in the following decade, it became apparent from studies of educational practice that individual decision-making was not the same as organisational decision-making. That created a way forward as well as a serious problem for the developing field.

Donald Schön went a long way towards bridging the personal–organisational gap with his highly innovative concept of "reflective practice": before you make a decision about a particular practice, be sure you have considered the practice in question from a range of perspectives, including those with contributing roles as well as yourself.

Schön's work represented a paradigm shift and was met with international acclaim.

But then another problem arose: What if the problem you are investigating defies rational analysis? What if it is a haphazard, unconventional issue that requires immediate attention? Does intuition on your part have a part to play in the decision process? If so, how? A new generation of scholars, such as Vroom and Yetton, responded with intriguing concepts such as "feedback loop": before finalising your decision, consider the likely impacts on key workplace processes and get reliable feedback from those who have a built-in interest.

Shortly after, Canadian Henry Mintzberg entered the fray with yet another innovative thought: that an important key in effective decision-making is efficient time management. In other words, build the element of time into your decision process and don't allow yourself to be unduly hurried. That concept was very helpful though not especially practical in situations of urgency (and school principals confronting duty of care issues often do not have the luxury of time on their side).

At about that same time, Americans Tannenbaum and Schmidt introduced yet another concept that was to have long-term impacts, namely, participative decision-making. Their contribution was quite new in educational thinking and was helped to gain credibility by the interesting flow charts that they and other researchers developed to assist with explanation.

It was at about this time, in the early 1970s, that I completed my Master of Education degree at one of the leading North American universities. I was certainly taken in by what, to me, was a powerful and exciting new concept, namely, reflective workplace decision-making. I returned to my principal's job full of enthusiasm.

I clearly recall my disillusionment when I found that my studies had limited practical value. They did not help much with the multifaceted issues that I confronted regularly. They were too linear, too removed from my daily routines and too unresponsive to criteria that I considered important, including student achievement and teacher wellbeing. I abandoned my interest in the study of educational administration, including decision-making, for the ensuing two decades.

In the early 1990s I embarked with colleagues from Education Queensland and the University of Southern Queensland on a national project (we called it the IDEAS Project) that sought to enhance teacher morale and professionalism at the same time as it enhanced pedagogical practice. I met Norm Hunter at about this time, and his questions about sustainable school quality seemed to be very much the same as mine. He was held in deep regard by his teacher colleagues, he was experimenting with powerful new forms of distributed leadership (including co-principalship) and he believed that sound educational practice had a strong scholarly base, and vice versa.

I touched bases with him on multiple occasions as the 1990s and early 2000s unfolded, and it is fair to say that the ground-breaking processes of the IDEAS Project gained strength, clarity and sustainability from Norm's always thoughtful critique and input. And as the IDEAS Project gained momentum, and international success, my interest in leader decision-making was rekindled. In fact it quickly became something of a passion, particularly when my books on schoolwide processes were well-received in the United States (which is where it had all begun but where, by 2000, there seemed to be something of a vacuum in innovative thinking).

So what came from our IDEAS Project across Australia and in several other countries that relates to this book?

One answer to that question is that decision-making is most effective when it occurs in the context of an authentic schoolwide vision, meaningful schoolwide values, culturally appropriate schoolwide pedagogy and responsive schoolwide leadership. "Consistency" is the word that I use to sum up these four integral components. It is a concept that recognises the work of Simon, Schön, Mintzberg and so forth – but extends their thinking into practical school processes, just as Norm Hunter has done.

A second answer to this question lies in the specific chapters, pages and topics of this superb book. What Norm has done, in a nutshell, is to re-open the lid of the Pandora's Box that Simon and Schön opened a half century ago, but that, in my view, has remained essentially closed, or at least half closed, since that time. Until now. This book is that exceptional. It is that significant. It is that good.

Each individual reader will select their own preferred chapter or concept. There are many very powerful concepts to select from. For me, speaking personally, the "power of hope" concept is especially appealing because, firstly, I have not previously seen it linked to decision-making as a process and, secondly, it is part and parcel of forms of school leadership that are widely thought to be the essence of positive schooling in today's world.

That is just one gem that we can take from Norm's reflections on a lifetime of outstanding educational practice. I encourage you to do what I have done since my reading of the final draft – select your own gem, then see how other key concepts in the book fit around it to give you new meaning and power in your own work. Follow the lead of Mintzberg, or Vroom and Yetton, and perhaps draw a diagram of what you come up with. You may find yourself landing in the same place as Norm Hunter. Rest assured that if you do, that would be a red letter day for the world of education.

Frank Crowther
June 2024

About the author

Norm Hunter likes to think of himself as a "pracademic". He practised as a primary teacher then secondary teacher, and was founding co-principal, with John Lindsay, then principal of Hillbrook Anglican School in Brisbane, serving for 21 years. He is a Fellow of both the Australian Council for Educational Leaders (ACEL) and the Australian College of Educators (ACE), and received the Queensland ACE Medal, "For distinguished, outstanding and continuing service to education at the school, state and national levels". He has also received ACEL's national Nganakarra Award ("presented annually to those whose general excellence in educational administration and whose learning, experience and contribution to the Council have earned lasting respect and gratitude") and the Medal of the Order of Australia for his contribution to educational leadership.

As his career in education evolved, he refined his values and beliefs, learnt from his successes and mistakes, and drew from research, including formal academic study and keeping up to date with professional reading. He has found that reading fiction complements and often enriches his formal professional reading, which you'll find evidenced in this book.

Norm now works as an educational leadership consultant and serves on the board of a non-profit educational foundation. He has served on a number of university leadership bodies and chaired or served on numerous educational committees, including two state-wide ministerial reviews. He guest-lectures to post-graduate students on educational leadership, continues to engage in professional reading, presents at conferences, and attends many professional learning opportunities.

Norm is an accomplished jazz pianist, having played in several big bands and in a mid-to-late-1960s rock band. He is married to Rae, and they have two daughters and four grandchildren.

Acknowledgements

A number of friends and colleagues generously responded to my request to offer their thoughts and advice on various drafts of the book. I thank Roger Hunter, Frank Crowther, Bruce Addison, Yvonne Hawke, Karen Fox, Pat Coughlan, Carol Nicoll, Alexander Mason, Yvonne Hill, Bob Hunter, Jacqui Zervos and John Pitman. Their advice and encouragement were invaluable, and I assure them they are all here in these pages, enriching what I was able to offer.

My thanks and appreciation to Alicia Cohen of Amba Press for her immediate and continuing support and encouragement for this book, and to my editor, Andrew Campbell, whose understanding of what I've tried to achieve and his suggestions to improve it have been invaluable.

Prologue

Each morning I receive a delivery of one of Australia's national newspapers. On a particular day during the writing of this book, the newly elected Australian Parliament was set to hold its first sitting in Canberra, the national capital. The letters section of the newspaper has a daily column of short, one or two sentence opinions expressed by readers. That morning one of them read:

> This Monday morning we were told the new government will be hitting the ground running. A few of us would prefer it hit the ground thinking. (Letter to *The Australian*, 26 July 2022)

In those few words, the letter writer has captured the essence of this book. It's about decision-making: perhaps the most important responsibility of leadership. It's an essential capability that all leaders – especially school leaders – need to develop to the highest possible level. To be more precise, this book is about *thinking* about decision-making: exploring the social and psychological milieu that is there in every decision, much of it invisible on the surface. I'm suggesting to you that a deep understanding of what is happening every time you go through a decision-making process will greatly enhance the decisions that emerge from that process.

This book is for educational leaders, whatever their context. Most of my examples and references come from education, because that's where I've lived and worked for so many years, but I'm confident there are learnings here that can inform and enrich the decision-making of leaders in any organisation.

At the very beginning, here's something to think about. I'll be offering what I believe to be wisdom from researchers, thinkers, writers and my own experiences. Here's one to whet your appetite: when making decisions, *why* you come to a particular decision in preference to other options is more important than *what* you do or *how* you do it. If that challenges your thinking, read on, and open your mind to more of the challenging ideas that follow. They will help you to make better decisions, and to feel more confident in the process of making them.

I'm confident that the learnings from the journey I'm inviting you to take with me will apply to varying leadership contexts: executive leaders, middle leaders, and non-positional leaders. Stay with that word "learnings". You're not going to find solutions or action plans in these pages. You'll get to those yourself in good time. I'm inviting you to pause on the action and engage in some learnings that involve deep thinking, going beyond where your current thinking might be.

We're all synthesisers, drawing our thoughts and ideas from many sources, and I'm no exception: ideas from here, ideas from there, sometimes from formal research, sometimes from poetry, novels, plays, music, dance or sport; sometimes from intuition, sometimes from experience, all merging into a unique and complex brew that we'll later explore as *mindscapes* or *mental models*.

I want to offer you a collection of ideas drawn from research, literature and experience that I believe haven't been brought together in this way before, and which, when synthesised, can offer meaning, wisdom, a sense of purpose, and some peace of mind to the way you make decisions in your school or system, and therefore to your leadership. You'll be navigating without a roadmap or global positioning system; just your own personal compass to guide you as we bring together ideas, thoughts and experiences, some of which I'm confident you won't have encountered before.

My hope is that as you read, you'll pause and take in the landscapes we travel through, consciously and unconsciously refine them through your natural intellectual and emotional filters, and store droplets of meaning and wisdom from each chapter. Let them build up, so when you've read the final chapter you'll find yourself with a portable wellspring of meaning and wisdom that you can drink from and be sustained by as you grapple with the most demanding responsibility you will face as an educational leader: decision-making.

Between the idea
And the reality ...

- *The assertion that the **why** that lies behind our decisions is more important than the **what** or the **how** comes from Simon Sinek, whom we'll meet further down the road. What was your first thought when you read it?*

"Here, on this paper, there are only you and me, and the things that each of us tries so hard to understand, clambering up through long, long researches into the past, and thinking ponderously and seeking, and finding that for which we looked a glorified question mark."

– John Steinbeck

CHAPTER I
A marijuana leaf and an octopus

It's late afternoon at River Valley High School. The leadership team – the principal, two deputy principals, and the business manager – are in deep conversation with an English teacher, the school counsellor, a student wellbeing teacher, and a teacher whose special responsibility is advising the school on keeping up to date with the legal and illegal drug scene.

Earlier this morning they were confronted with a difficult situation. The Year 11 English classes have just completed a unit entitled "Where Do I Stand?", where students were asked to choose a controversial issue in society, research its background, explain the arguments for and against, and then take a position one way or the other, justifying their view.

Emily is a Year 11 student who is highly regarded by teachers and students. She is a high achiever, feisty and mature, and often a strong contributor to class discussions. Before school, Emily's English teacher arrived at the principal's door with an assignment in her hand and a worried look on her face. She quickly handed the assignment to the principal, and with a sigh of relief and a sympathetic smile said, "Now it's your problem."

For the assignment, Emily has chosen to research the issue of legalisation of marijuana, and in the spirit of creative presentation and with a touch of her characteristic feistiness, she has glued a real marijuana leaf on the cover page of her assignment. She is now technically in breach of the school's drugs policy, which includes the statement, "Anyone in possession of an illegal substance at school, or who brings an illegal substance onto the school property, must expect to leave the school".

It is indeed now the principal's problem. He is responsible to the school board, to the school's students in general and to Emily in particular; he is responsible for the reputation of the school in the wider community, and he also has duty-of-care responsibilities through the civil and criminal laws of the state of Queensland, which, at the time, were strongly punitive on illegal drugs, including marijuana.

It's important to note here that in Australia, if a school operates under participative or democratic decision-making and leadership, that is the choice of the principal. It's a cultural artefact, not structural. Australian schools have clear organisational structures, but whether their cultures are democratic, participative or autocratic is an internal issue for each school. Hence the weight that now rests on the River Valley High's principal as he ponders the nuances of his duty of care: to Emily, to the other students, and to the school.

Clearly this is not black and white or one-dimensional, nor is it just about one student. How it is resolved will impact on how the school is perceived by its own community, and will influence perceptions in the wider community, because word gets around quickly in this part of the world. In a sense, for the principal and school leadership team, the eyes of the world are on them: this is going to tax their decision-making capabilities to the limit.

*

Not long ago I watched the movie *My Octopus Teacher*. It's a fascinating, true story told by Craig Foster, a free-diver who explores the underwater environment of a cove near Cape Town, South Africa. Foster has mastered the skill of free-diving, and during his underwater explorations he has slowly and patiently developed a relationship with an octopus: a relationship in which the octopus has come to recognise him, and in its own way to welcome him into its world. Equally fascinating is that world itself: the octopus lives in a literal "underworld", invisible from the surface, with its own unique ecology.

Foster's visits begin on the calm waters on the surface of the cove, which the camera takes in. Then the camera goes with him as he enters the underwater world of the octopus. In astonishing contrast to the calm, uncomplicated view from the surface, the camera captures a vibrant, complex world of forests, pathways and caves, populated by a great variety of living creatures, some living in harmony with one another, some in competition with one another, and others preying on more vulnerable inhabitants. The more Foster explores this world beneath the surface the more he learns and understands. And he finds that some of these learnings and understandings impact on his life above the surface.

In order to spend extended time in that world before having to return to the surface, Foster spent many months of preparation, gradually building on his ability to conserve his breath, which enabled him to spend time slowly developing his relationship with the octopus, and taking in the complexity and nuance of the world beneath the surface. He didn't just dive in, look around, and return to the surface. Without taking the time to do the preparation for free-diving, he couldn't have taken in the richness of that world. It brought him to a level of understanding and fulfilment he hadn't experienced before.

My Octopus Teacher could serve as a metaphor for what I'm inviting you to think about in this book. I've learnt that what we see on the surface of a school is a fraction of what is actually happening in it. If you don't understand this and take it into account when making decisions, you're going to miss important things, including opportunities and threats that are waiting beneath the surface whether you look for them or not. This book is for those who want to look: and if you're in a school leadership role, I'm suggesting you need to look.

That means preparing – in this case pausing and taking the time to refine and prioritise your thinking before acting. If that goes against your understanding of what leadership and decision-making are about, you have a choice. You can stop reading now because you're too busy for this; you have a to-do list, important decisions to make, and you don't have time for the luxury of engaging in a thinkfest when there's work to be done. Or you can pause and consider whether the time Craig Foster took to master free-diving, and the meaning and wisdom that investment brought to him about his own world, might hint at something worth pursuing here: indeed, something you might choose to pursue if you're going to be an authentic and effective school leader. Read on … or don't.

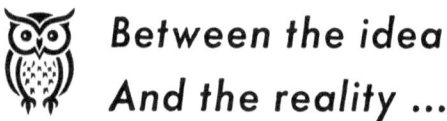
Between the idea
And the reality ...

- *Stand in the River Valley principal's shoes for a moment when the teacher hands him Emily's assignment. What are the first thoughts that come into your mind? Jot them down, because it will be interesting to see how they compare with your thoughts when you've finished reading this book.*
- *Try to find the time to watch* My Octopus Teacher. *It's an uplifting story, and a great way of conceptualising what we're embarking on here.*

CHAPTER 2
The age of ambiguity

"For every complex issue there's always an answer that is clear and simple – and it's always wrong." – H. L. Mencken

We often hear calls for leadership that is "decisive", "quick thinking", "action-oriented" or "solutions-focused", and we need to recognise that for what it usually means: a quick fix. We know from research and experience that quick fixes rarely work, and purely intuitive judgements leading to quick decisions are often a recipe for failure, and possibly disaster (e.g., Senge et al., 2000).

I need to acknowledge early on that quick and decisive decisions are sometimes needed, usually in crisis or military combat situations. Both those exceptions to what I'm offering are important and valid, but each is a book on its own. I'm writing about decisions in schools and education systems that range from strategic to day-to-day; and sometimes it's hard to tell one from the other.

I don't wish to complicate the already difficult work of leadership. At the same time, we must accept that we live in a world of complexity and uncertainty, and we have available research, thinking, wisdom and experience that have been evolving for some time now. I'm inviting you to bundle up your own experience and intuition, your values and beliefs, take a deep breath, and free-dive into that research, experience and thinking. A warning: like Craig Foster, you'll need to learn to hold your breath and explore beneath the surface for some time before surfacing.

*

I believe we can accurately describe the times we're living in as "The age of ambiguity".

> **ambiguity**: doubtfulness or uncertainty of meaning; equivocal; open to various interpretations (*Macquarie Dictionary*, 2001).
>
> **ambiguity**: difficult to comprehend, distinguish or classify; obscure; of uncertain significance (*Penguin English Dictionary*, 2002).

The definitions from these two dictionaries elegantly capture what we're talking about here, and why all this is so relevant, because whatever takes place in the societies of the wider world is always reflected in some way in the schools and education systems within those societies. And much of it is beneath the surface: invisible, but impacting on the work of those who lead and make decisions.

Language reflects reality

At the outset we need to acknowledge that the age of ambiguity hasn't suddenly arrived out of nowhere. It's actually been evolving for centuries, and during those years leaders like you and me have struggled to make meaning and glean wisdom from what is happening around them, especially when the status quo is being disturbed. They have tried to make sense of what constitutes "reality" and "truth", and as the world has become increasingly complex, we are now at a point in history where there is little agreement in western societies about what "reality" and "truth" even mean. And that finds its way into our organisations, including our universities, schools and systems, and into our minds. If we're going to lead, we have to find ways to make meaning and sense of it for our school communities.

For all of this century and the second half of the previous one, our understanding of management, leadership and decision-making has been changing in ways that reflect this evolution. An example of this is the way the language describing particular university post-graduate courses in education has changed over a relatively short time. In the 1960s–80s the term mainly used for those courses was "administration"; in the 1990s it was "management'; and as we moved into the 2000s "leadership" became more widely used, with some researchers seeing distinctions between leadership and management, and others seeing them as inseparable: two parts of an integrated whole. Those changes in language represent a deepening of our understanding and conceptualisation, moving from the fairly benign "administration" to the more powerful and proactive "leadership". Words affect our thoughts, and thoughts affect our actions.

I'm suggesting that if you're going to be an educational leader making decisions in the age of ambiguity, you need to have a considered, personal view of what leadership and management mean to you, and most importantly, why you hold those views, because that flows directly into the decisions you make for those you aspire to lead. If you are in a current leadership role, that's happening right now, every day, whether you've consciously thought about it or not. And if it's happening right now, every day, it really is important that you take time to consciously think about it.

Find the words that capture your own conceptualising of leadership, and be able to stretch out on it with colleagues, explaining it, defending it and perhaps modifying it. I'm offering this book as a catalyst for you to do this more clearly and confidently than you might have done before. It relates directly to the quality of your decision-making; and as we'll see, it involves the head, the heart, and the hand of what it means to be an educational leader – especially a school leader.

*

The changes in language for university post-graduate courses are indicative of the research and thinking that have been challenging historic assumptions about leadership; in particular the quick-thinking, action-oriented, solutions-focused model, and also the idea that leaders are born, not made. This more recent thinking suggests that leadership is more complex than was previously thought, and can be studied and learnt. These challenges to previous assumptions about leadership are important, and they apply directly to decision-making. At the same time, notwithstanding these recent learnings, much research, writing and thinking from the past also offer insights for today.

We're about to go back and explore this evolving process, pausing along the way to delve deeply into the world that lies beneath the surface of every decision every leader makes. We'll see that what might appear on the surface to be simple situations with simple solutions often turn out be subtle, nuanced and complicated in ways that are not easy to see and understand on a first look. Indeed, failure by leaders to grasp this has often led to ineffective and sometimes disastrous decisions – like the one that follows.

The rats of Hanoi

Jason Murphy relates an example of leaders assuming a situation was quite simple and that what was needed was therefore a simple solution. In 1890, in the French colony that was then part of Indochina (now the nations of Vietnam, Laos and Cambodia), the authorities decided to create healthier living conditions by constructing sewers beneath Hanoi. They were particularly concerned about the possible spread of disease. The engineering of the project was highly successful, but there was one problem: the sewers soon attracted rats, which did what rats do and began to reproduce quickly and in large numbers. Fearing the spread of diseases like bubonic plague and typhoid, the French authorities quickly and decisively initiated what they thought was a clever solution. They introduced an incentive scheme encouraging the locals to kill rats, paying money for every rat tail presented as evidence.

The locals responded with enthusiasm, soon presenting so many tails that the French authorities began to wonder if there could really be so many rats in the sewers. On investigation, they found that not only were rats being killed in the sewers, but the locals had also established a business model based on rat-breeding farms, which had quickly developed into a thriving industry all over Hanoi, giving the French authorities what they wanted and creating a steady income for the locals.

When the authorities discovered what was happening, they shut down the scheme, resulting in thousands of now unsaleable rats being released and invading the city. Within a few months, bubonic plague made its appearance in Hanoi (Murphy, 2019).

So what went wrong? Clearly, what appeared to be simple wasn't simple at all. The French decision-makers failed to understand what lay beneath the surface (apart from sewers): what they saw as a structural health issue was to the locals, who were largely living in poverty, a cultural and economic issue with an attractive incentive that they could easily act on for their own benefit.

As we'll continue to explore in the following chapters, the human factor – usually expressed through culture rather than structure – is always at work when decisions are made, and it's often unpredictable, especially if simplistic assumptions are made leading to quick, decisive action. And the danger of unintended outcomes is especially high when decisions are made in that way. As Murphy's example shows, with their quick and decisive decision the French authorities unintentionally set in train consequences that brought about the very situation they were trying to prevent.

Simple or simplistic?

Some leaders have opted to interpret complexity, uncertainty and nuance by not interpreting them, clinging to simplistic assumptions about leadership and organisations that never worked beyond the "quick fix" and are unlikely to work in the age of ambiguity. Leadership is not a simple skill and never was, and trying to believe that it is will likely end in tears. At the same time, I'm suggesting that you can use simple – as distinct from simplistic – concepts and strategies to make meaning and find wisdom and purpose amid complexity and uncertainty.

> ... you can use simple – as distinct from simplistic – concepts and strategies to make meaning and find wisdom and purpose amid complexity and uncertainty.

The young contemporary musician and educator Jacob Collier provides an excellent example of seeking ways to understand complexity that are simple, but not simplistic:

> The way I've thought about music has deepened and simplified. I think it started on a ravenously fascinated level, trying to understand really deep and crazy concepts. Over the years, I'm getting more and more of a hefty kick out of something being done so beautifully, with all of the depth that supports it from the rich and complex world, but actually expressed in an incredibly simple way. (Collier in McMillen, 2022, p. 5)

Like Collier, I'm a musician – a jazz pianist – and like him I'm also an educational leader. Some of my deepest insights about leadership have come from my involvement with music and musicians, and I see much in common with Collier's thinking – if only I'd had such insights when I was his age (and had his talent at the piano)!

A music lesson

Join me now as we take a seat at a jazz concert. The essence of playing jazz is the art and science of music improvisation. Often musicians improvising on a piece of music look relaxed, or "cool", and it appears they're just making it up as they go along. They're not. Nor are they relaxed. They're constantly making decisions about what to play based on the framework of the piece they're playing – the structure, the chord progressions, the melody, the rhythm, and if it's a song, the lyric. All the musicians in the band have that same framework in their heads or on a page in front of them. The individual musicians who take their turn to improvise on the piece are bringing their unique take on it, but each of them is making musical decisions based on the shared context of that common and agreed framework. That's why it can generate such creativity from the players yet still hold together, and why it's so satisfying for a discerning listener, and for the musicians themselves, who are contributing to something bigger than their own individual input.

Sometimes during this continuous decision-making process a problem presents itself, especially if the piece being performed is complex in its structure. If even one of the musicians mistakenly strays from the common framework, the integrity of the group performance is threatened. But the performance doesn't fall apart, because the agreed framework enables the other band members to quickly cover for the mistake and bring the piece back to where it should be. Some are so skilled at this that the audience doesn't even realise that a mistake was made: the soloist and the band members find each other so smoothly because their shared understanding of the framework is so strong. It's collaboration at the highest level: a clear, agreed structure acted out through a culture combining individualism and collaboration. And it's the cultural component that is the key to the performance.

One of the most often-cited examples of this combination of group coherence and individual creativity is Miles Davis's album *Kind of Blue*. The band is a sextet, so it needed teamwork along with self-expression. Davis had prepared "sketches" of the pieces to be performed. The agreed framework was there, but he left a lot of space for the band members to contribute their ideas. Frank Barrett suggests that Davis's approach to leading the *Kind of Blue* session hinged on him never being overly attached to his own ideas. He offered ideas to see where they might lead, but he was never defensive about them. They were there to spark players' imagination, to get their ideas going.

Barrett's understanding of Davis's approach to leadership is insightful:

> Leaders like this know that they don't create great things alone. They concoct directions to get things moving, and they don't expect that

all of them will work out. If a better idea emerges as a result, it's not a failure ... What makes these interventions powerful is that the leader holds a positive image of what others are capable of. This often means seeing other people's strengths better than they see their own strengths. (Barrett, 2012, p. 147)

So when playing jazz, the band members know that while each of them is encouraged to interpret the piece in a personally distinctive way, they are all working within the same shared structure; and here's the thing: when structure and culture are complementary, the whole becomes greater than the sum of the parts. Such a simple concept, but such a long way from simplistic; and I'm sure that's what Jacob Collier is talking about when he says the music is both "deepened and simplified".

There's a powerful metaphor here, and the further we explore it, the more I think you'll see its relevance to educational leadership and decision-making.

A deeply human exercise

Does that thinking expedition spark something in your mind about decision-making and leadership? The conceptual evolution of leadership over the years pushes us toward a more sophisticated appreciation of what lies at the core of the art and science of decision-making, and the more it evolves the more the importance of the human factor imposes itself into structures, systems, strategies and plans. From what might appear to be ordinary day-to-day decisions through to the deeper and longer-term work of devising a strategic plan, striving to build a shared framework, or forging an organisational culture, I'm asking you to accept this "reality" and "truth": whether in a school or any other organisation, leadership is a deeply human exercise. We'll be taking a lot of time to stretch out on this fundamental understanding about decision-making, and in particular its relationship to school leadership.

Efficient and effective?

It's true that time is something school leaders have to use efficiently. But there is a corollary to that: your time also has to be used effectively. The best way to achieve both in your decision-making is to take the time to think in ways in which you may not have thought before. Are you brave enough to step back for a while from the busy work on your to-do list and do a second to-do list with one entry: *Create some thinking time*?

> *Are you brave enough to step back for a while from the busy work on your to-do list and do a second to-do list with one entry:*
> Create some thinking time?

If you can commit to this, it's likely that you're going to make many more good decisions than bad ones. And you'll find wisdom, meaning, and a sense of purpose, and build resilience for yourself and your organisation to see you through difficult times, including the mistakes that you, and every school leader, will inevitably make. As you engage in perhaps the most complex work in society today – that of educational leadership in the age of ambiguity – it's my hope that thinking about this and discussing it with your colleagues will draw some simplicity out of the complexity, and help you to bring meaning and wisdom to the unique context of the school or system you lead.

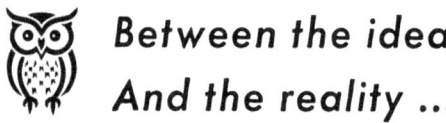

- *What do you think about the difference between "simple" and "simplistic"? Please give it some thought, because it's important to what follows.*
- *Many researchers are drawing a distinction between "leadership" and "management". Do you see a difference? What are your thoughts about this?*
- *Listen to Miles Davis's 1984 recording of Cindi Lauper's "Time After Time". Listen to Cindi, then listen to Miles. Can you hear how the jazz musicians bring their own interpretations into the performance, but are all working together on the shared and agreed structure of the song, preserving its essence?*

CHAPTER 3
A long and winding road

"I believe finally that education must be conceived as a continuing reconstruction of experience; that the process and the goal of education are one and the same thing." – John Dewey

Leadership: positional or … ?

In exploring what lies beneath the surface of decision-making today, I've learnt that there's a lot there. It's especially important at this early stage to be clear that in our conceptualising of leadership, "leaders" includes positional leadership, but goes beyond that to what is commonly called "distributed leadership". That's part of a deeper understanding of how decision-making and leadership work in schools and education systems. We have known for some time that there are teachers and indeed support staff in schools and systems who clearly lead, often through positive contributions to decision-making or to what lies behind decision-making: the culture of the school or system. It's the same in every organisation.

This has been widely recognised and acknowledged in research, and is demonstrably important (e.g., Crowther et al., 2002, 2021; Fullan, 2020; Hagstrom, 2004; MacBeath, 2004; MacBeath et al., 2003; Marquet, 2015; Palmer, 2007). So while it applies to leaders in all organisations, distributed leadership has particular relevance for those who honour the profession of teaching by stepping up and leading in our schools, including those who lead in non-positional roles, often undervalued, and at times invisible, to everyone but themselves.

"The silence in our mind"

It might surprise you, but I'm entrusting solutions, strategic plans, and action plans to your own capable hands, in your own context. In the spirit of John Dewey's words above, it's in your *thinking* about those things that I'm inviting you, indeed urging you, to delve beneath the surface: to engage in what we know from research and experience is likely to lead to more good decisions than bad ones. It involves exploring and articulating how you conceptualise leadership in general and for yourself in particular, placing that in the context of today's world, and then on into your decision-making in your own school or system. And it's not a one-off exercise: as John Dewey says above, it's a continuing element in the process of educational leadership.

To get your thinking juices working, here is the Nobel Prize-winning psychologist and cognitive scientist Daniel Kahneman introducing something of the complexity and nuance involved in exploring how our thinking impacts on the decisions we make:

> When you are asked what you are thinking about, you can normally answer. You believe you know what goes on in your mind, which often consists of one conscious thought leading in an orderly way to another. But that is not the only way the mind works, nor indeed is that the typical way. Most impressions and thoughts arise in your own conscious experience without your knowing how they got there ... The mental work that produces impressions, intuitions and many decisions goes on in silence in our mind. (Kahneman, 2012, p. 4)

The mental work that produces impressions, intuitions and many decisions goes on in silence in our mind.

We'll explore that "silence in our mind" in some depth later, because it has important implications for the way school leaders make decisions. But for now, we return to the big picture.

*

Please accept that we're not travelling on a jet aircraft or a fast train. We're walking on a long and winding road, and you're sketching for yourself the unique maps that underpin your decision-making. It's an exploratory road trip with no pre-packaged solutions. The good news is, much of what you need for the journey is already there in your head and heart: in your values, beliefs, feelings, intuition and experience. And mine are there too, accompanying you. Part of it involves finding what's already there, and then finding the words to articulate it. You'll build on it through the richness of research, which you'll synthesise and apply specifically to yourself in your own unique context; and the further good news is that it will ultimately have a powerful impact on your decision-making, and therefore on the quality of your leadership.

We're travelling through places you may well have visited before, but this time we'll pause, take a deep breath, and look beneath the surface, taking in the ambience of the surroundings, using the opportunity to find meaning, wisdom and purpose as we go: for yourself, for your colleagues, and for the school you lead. And as we go, I think you'll find that, as Dewey suggests, the process and the goal will begin to merge.

We begin by going back a few hundred years, and it may seem at first to be just history. It *is* history, but it's more than that, and I hope you'll see that it relates to your leadership work right now, today. People have walked this road before, and they have explored what it means to be human, and what it means to lead and make decisions in complex and uncertain times. We're doing the same thing, respectfully reflecting on it in ways that are simple, but not simplistic. Be patient, pause on the "busy work" calling you to action, and take some time now as we explore where these tracks have come from. And they come from a long way back.

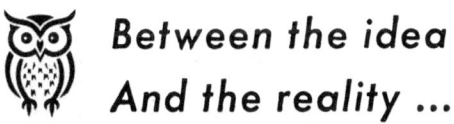
Between the idea
And the reality ...

- *Is there a thought or idea in what you've read so far that you can relate to in your decision-making processes in your organisation? Stretch out on it with your colleagues.*
- *Engage your colleagues in a conversation about what John Dewey might be getting at in the quote that introduced this chapter.*

CHAPTER 4

Going back ... to go forward

"If you don't know where you've come from, you don't know where you're going." – Maya Angelou, poet; Jerry Coker, jazz musician

Time travelling

Just north of Sydney, on the banks of the Dyarubbin–Hawkesbury River, there is a sandstone rock platform with pictures etched into it by people whose heritage in the area can be traced back 60,000 years. It's an ancient diorama depicting wildlife including emus, kangaroos and birds. Along with them is a faded though still recognisable representation of a three-masted sailing ship. In etching the image of that ship into the sandstone all those years ago, were the artists simply recording something they had seen, or did they also perhaps have a premonition that this was a portent of something significant, perhaps ominous?

After visiting the site, Australian historian Anna Clark was moved to write:

> ... the "contact zones" of colonial forays into the New Worlds of the Americas and the Pacific weren't simply physical spaces but also metaphysical, where different peoples, cultures and beliefs clashed, clamoured and came together. (Clark, 2022, p. 22)

We can never know what went through the minds of the people who stood watching a ship sailing up the east coast of their country in 1770, with towering sails, crewed by men with white faces and wearing strange clothing. Did those watchers sense that not just their ways of life but, as Anna Clark suggests, their existential worldviews, were going to be challenged and perhaps changed forever? Maybe, maybe not, but it's likely that some felt an uneasiness, others a sense of anxiety, or some bewilderment, about what the arrival of those strangers in that strange ship might mean for them.

In the 1940s it was rare for Indigenous writers to be published in Australia. At the time, two non-Indigenous researchers were trying to capture what the arrival of the Europeans might have meant in words drawn from conversations with Aboriginal people. W. E. Harney devoted his life to promoting the cause of Australia's Indigenous people, and his colleague, A. P. Elkin, was an anthropologist and university professor who, in the words of the *University of Sydney News*, "played a large part in creating a new public attitude to Aborigines" (Williams, 1970).

Harney and Elkin published *Songs of the Songman* in 1949. With no written language to draw from, they had gathered and documented songs and stories from Aboriginal men and women over many years, then retold them in writing.

Listen to the words of one of those songs:

> Poor fellow me, poor fellow me,
> My country it gave me
> All that I see.
> Gifts that I see, all that I see,
> Poor fellow me ...
>
> Now I'm alone, now I'm alone,
> Nothing I own, spirit has flown.
> Poor fellow me.

Separated from his tribe and his country, it seems that this man's life has lost meaning. The enormous change that has impacted on him and his people means that his "spirit has flown", and now it seems he has nothing to live for.

On the other side of the world, in the exact same year that Aboriginal people watched the *Endeavour* sail up the east coast of "the great south land", Oliver Goldsmith's poem "The Deserted Village" was published in England. The massive changes to people's lives wrought by the Industrial Revolution were becoming evident, and Goldsmith was lamenting the upheaval for rural village life and the natural countryside. At one point, Goldsmith remembers the village preacher:

> At church, with meek and unaffected grace,
> His looks adorned the venerable place;
> Truth from his lips prevailed with double sway,
> And fools who came to scoff remained to pray.

For Goldsmith, the stability, the certainty, "the truth" as revealed through the village preacher's sermons, are gone, as is the beauty of the countryside. Instead:

> Here as I take my solitary rounds,
> Amidst thy tangling walks and ruined grounds
> And, many a year elapsed, return to view
> Where once the cottage stood, the hawthorn grew,
> Remembrance wakes with all her busy train,
> Swells at my breast, and turns the past to pain.

Two hundred and fifty years ago, in the same year, on opposite sides of the world, people of vastly different histories and cultures were beginning to experience a similar sense of uncertainty, pain and loss that is hard to put into words, but involved feelings, intellect, and indeed their spiritual wellbeing, in response to change and anxiety about the future. For both, "spirit has flown".

*

You may be wondering how this can have anything to do with decision-making by school leaders today. I assure you it does. We're following a train of thought and related themes that lead us on a journey, looking at where we've come from to more clearly think about where we want to go. And that's important, as a senior scientist and professor of psychology at the University of Toronto recently reminded organisational leaders:

> From an evolutionary perspective, the purpose of memory … is not to allow us to sit back and say "Oh, do you remember that time?" It really is to help us make decisions. (Sheena Josselyn in Purtell, 2022)

Based on her research about memory, Josselyn asserts that there is a direct link between how we remember the past, and our decision-making in the present. We'll develop this further when we explore the nature of intuition in a later chapter; for now, I'm suggesting that for school leaders there is something important to learn from the past about making decisions today, and we would be wise to take note of it.

*

A hundred and forty years after "The Deserted Village" was published, after "the war to end all wars" had wrought unimagined death and destruction, the Irish poet W. B. Yeats tried to find words to capture the prevailing climate in the years following the First World War. His poem "The Second Coming" begins:

> The falcon cannot hear the falconer;
> Things fall apart; the centre cannot hold;
> Mere anarchy is loosed upon the world,
> The blood-dimmed tide is loosed, and everywhere
> The ceremony of innocence is drowned …

Almost 20 years later in 1938, with words less dramatic than those of Yeats, but just as poignant, French philosopher Jean-Paul Sartre published *Nausea*. It was another year that saw the world languishing in a state of uncertainty and anxiety, many experiencing an underlying fear that no-one knew how to deal with, let alone lead the way forward. While Yeats had looked beyond himself to the wider world, Sartre was looking within:

> Something has happened to me: I can't doubt that any more. It came as an illness does, not like an ordinary certainty, not like anything obvious. It installed itself cunningly, little by little; I felt a little strange, a little awkward, and that was all. Once it was established, it didn't move any more, it lay low and I was able to persuade myself that there was nothing wrong with me, that it was a false alarm. And now it has started blossoming … And there it is: since then, the nausea hasn't left me, it holds me in its grip. (Sartre, 1974, pp. 13, 33)

In the following year, Sartre's "nausea" and the widespread insecurity that people had been experiencing would prove to be prescient; tragically, "the war to end all wars" was not the war to end all wars, and the world was plunged into even greater death and destruction than that of 1914–18.

And again, amid change, uncertainty and anxiety, people wondered: Will the centre hold? Will the falcon again be able to hear the falconer? Will the nausea go away?

Just over 30 years after *Nausea* was published, and exactly 200 years after the *Endeavour* appeared off the east coast of the great south land and people in England were reading "The Deserted Village", Alvin Toffler published *Future Shock*. It was the time of the Vietnam War, the American civil rights movement, the Beatles and the "British Invasion", Woodstock and Haight-Ashbury, the feminist revolution, and major mechanisation of the workplace. Toffler writes:

> Much that now strikes us as incomprehensible would be far less so if we took a fresh look at the racing rate of change that makes reality seem, sometimes, like a kaleidoscope run wild. … It is a concrete force that reaches deep into our personal lives, compels us to act out new roles,

and confronts us with the danger of a new and powerfully upsetting psychological disease. This new disease can be called "future shock", and a knowledge of its source and symptoms helps explain many things that otherwise defy rational analysis. (Toffler, 1970, p. 19)

Toffler was one of the first to try to find meaning and make sense of the times in the years following the Second World War. Note his reference to "reality". He offered concepts and language to put forward the view that we need to understand and accept future shock and learn to live with it, because there is no going back to simpler times. He was saying that change is different now (1970), because it's accelerating over shorter periods of time. He was also suggesting that it was not necessarily a negative phenomenon: there were positives there that we should be identifying and harnessing. That's a theme to hold on to, and we'll return to it later.

Almost 30 years after the publication of *Future Shock*, as the world, particularly the workplace, was beginning to be further changed as mechanisation expanded into computer technology, James Gleick wrote in *Faster*:

> As we surround ourselves with quick technologies, we sometimes begin to doubt ourselves. We measure ourselves against our machines, and we worry that we are lagging behind. They are faster than we are. A poor human can't keep up. (Gleick, 1999, p. 119)

And:

> We make choices, but we have a sense that our choosing is not entirely free. We're like unvaccinated travellers through territory awash in disease. (p. 277)

That simile – "like unvaccinated travellers through territory awash with disease" – was especially pertinent as the world worked through the uncertainty and anxiety wrought by the unexpected onset of the Covid-19 virus.

Finally (for now), 20 or more years on from *Faster*, digital technology is integral to the workplace and artificial intelligence has added a further dimension. Moreover, we're living in an age of contesting perspectives on identity, religion, race, sexuality, gender and climate change, to name just some, all magnified through the ubiquitous, undisciplined impact of social media, which for many has replaced formal news reporting and any sense of reflective thinking. It's the post-modern world, but its nature has now shifted further than anyone could ever have imagined.

The Canadian educational researcher and writer Michael Fullan writes:

> In complex, what I have called chaotic times, leaders must be able to operate under conditions that are not always clear – worse, not as clear as they appear to be … "Coping with wildness lying in wait" may not be a bad job description for leading in a culture of change. (Fullan, 2020, p. xii)

And:

> I also have to say that humans face one enormous obstacle that no other beings face, namely **learning anxiety** – specifically, anxiety when it comes to learning something new. (p. 16)

(Fullan's reference to "coping with wildness lying in wait' is drawn from writing by G. K. Chesterton in *Orthodoxy*, 1908.)

Fifty years apart, are Toffler and Fullan exploring the same thing? Fast-moving change, disruption, complexity, anxiety and uncertainty continue to impose themselves on our lives and pose challenges for our personal, social and working lives, including in our psychological dispositions. The simple reality that leaders, especially school leaders, have to face is that we are in the age of ambiguity. It's been evolving for some time; to ignore it and not seek to understand it and make meaning from it is simplistic, and those who choose that road will almost certainly at some point come face to face with "the wildness lying in wait".

Change, disruption, complexity, uncertainty ... and consistency

We've just done some significant time-travelling, spanning approximately 250 years. Let's pause now and draw some learning and wisdom from it.

Firstly, those 250 years have seen change and disruption aplenty, some of it revolutionary, including the beginning and end of European colonialism, industrialisation, urbanisation, two world wars, a worldwide economic depression and several global recessions, massive change in the workplace, including the arrival of mechanisation, automation and artificial intelligence, the feminist movement, the fall of the Berlin Wall and with it the Soviet Union, the end of apartheid in South Africa, the rise of Islamist terrorism, identity politics, climate change, a pandemic that has affected every country in the world, Russia's invasion of Ukraine in 2022, and in October 2023 Hamas's attack on Israel and Israel's response.

Secondly, amid the change, disruption and uncertainty described by those writers we've been referencing, can you detect recurring themes across the years? Do you begin to get a sense of the implications for schools, systems and their leaders?

When we reflect on those writings, we begin to find lengthy threads weaving their way through the apparent confusion: complexity, disorder, fear, things incomprehensible, anxiety, worry, and feeling threatened by things that are happening and the way they are happening. We find references to illness, disease – including psychological disease – and pain, various ways of expressing uncertainty, doubt, loss and vulnerability, feelings of alienation and loss of meaning and hope: all happening at an increasing pace, and all ominously summed up in that phrase from G. K. Chesterton: *wildness lying in wait*.

Toffler refers to things that "defy rational analysis"; for Fullan things are "not as clear as they appear to be". Yet perhaps most relevant for us today is Goldsmith's pining for the loss of "truth" as conveyed by the village preacher, who brought reassurance and peace of mind to the congregation and converted "fools" who were previously ignorant of the "truth"; and this loss causes him "pain": clearly psychological pain.

Thirdly, important as it is to note the anxiety and sense of loss revealed in much of the writing, it's important to note that these writings are not just a series of laments and complaints. There is also wisdom, and most importantly, a common theme of people bravely struggling to make decisions: to make sense of things and find the words to explain meaning and purpose in the midst of apparent confusion. That's where we're going now.

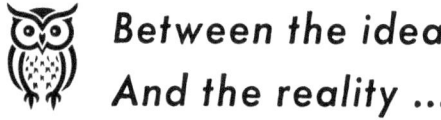

Between the idea
And the reality ...

- *One of the themes throughout this chapter has been the striving by writers and thinkers to find the words to make sense of what they are experiencing. Are there words or phrases used by any of these writers that resonated with you as you read this chapter? If so, why did they resonate?*

CHAPTER 5

Just what the truth is ...

> "A few decades back we wondered if we could handle the truth, now we struggle to find it." – Chris Kenny (2023)

Let's draw the previous chapters together and juxtapose the words of Goldsmith's village preacher, where "truth from his lips prevailed", with Toffler's linking of two words: "reality" and "seem". Isn't reality what is real and true? Surely it doesn't "seem" – it *is*. What Goldsmith was lamenting, and what Toffler was suggesting, is that we can no longer make that assumption. As we can see, this has been evolving for over 200 years, and we are now living in the post-modern world – the age of ambiguity – where everything is contestable, including "reality" and "truth". We are in unsettled territory: territory where more than 50 years ago, in 1967, the Beatles sang "Nothing is real" and the Moody Blues lamented, "Just what the truth is, I can't say any more". You could argue that it's superficial to quote from popular music when making a serious case, but popular music sometimes reflects its times; and the thing is, people listening to the radio didn't see those lines as particularly unusual for the times; in fact, some would say they were representative of the times. When Bob Dylan wrote "The times they are a-changing" in 1965, he was expressing something widely felt.

And 60 years later, the times are still a-changing. Making decisions in an age where for many people there is uncertainty, confusion, and at times conflict about fundamental principles like truth and reality is a tough call, but school leaders will find themselves sooner or later facing situations where they're going to have to define those concepts in order to make a decision and then explain it and have it accepted by their school community. That is the challenge the River Valley High principal and leadership team are facing with Emily's marijuana leaf.

"Alternate facts"

You'll have picked up by now that my point is: at a deeper level none of this is new. Goldsmith saw that the nature of "truth" was already being challenged in 1770. Fast forward just under 180 years from then to another writer who wrote to make sense of what he was experiencing. George Orwell's *1984* was published in 1947. The hero of the story, Winston Smith, is a public servant working in the Department of Truth. Winston's job is to research historical documents, including books and news reports, and to remove any references that vary from the government's official version of what happened in the past. The mission of the Department of Truth is, in fact, to lie: to destroy all evidence of what happened in the past and create a false story of particular events for the public, declaring it as the "real" truth.

We're returning to the power of words, and in 1947 Orwell was prophetic. In January 2017, 70 years after the publication of *1984*, the newly-elected United States President made the claim that the number of people who had attended his presidential inauguration a few weeks earlier was greater than that of his predecessor. When presented at a media conference with official data showing that the claim was false, the White House spokesperson responded that she was presenting "alternate facts". She was asserting that, despite data demonstrating otherwise, there are different versions of the truth, with the implication that people can choose whichever version they prefer. Four years later, the same president claimed that he had won the 2020 presidential election, despite validated data showing that he hadn't. He had presented another "alternate fact", and here's the important learning to take from it: millions of people believed it, despite the evidence showing it was untrue. Not so long ago, "alternate facts" would have been seen as an oxymoron. No longer. And this is not an isolated example regarding one person. It's indicative of something more widespread: the manipulation of language to suit particular purposes.

This shouldn't really surprise us. Like so much that we've already looked at, it isn't new. And like so much of what we've already looked at, there's wisdom and insight about this in literary sources. One example: couched in humour, the potential for using words to create "alternate facts" was addressed 150 years ago. First published in 1872, Lewis Carroll's *Alice in Wonderland*

and *Through the Looking-Glass*, like the work of Aesop and Hans Christian Andersen, were, and still are, widely seen as children's books. But they aren't. They are deliberately disguised as fairy tales, but their wisdom and insight are directed at adults. Look at the exchange below between Humpty Dumpty and Alice in the fantasy world beyond the Looking Glass:

> "When I use a word", Humpty Dumpty said, in a rather scornful tone, "it means just what I choose it to mean – neither more nor less."
>
> "The question is," said Alice, "whether you **can** make words mean so many different things."
>
> "The question is," said Humpty Dumpty, "which is to be master – that's all." (Carroll, 1998, p. 186)

Look again at Humpty's words. There's arrogance in his "rather scornful tone" to Alice, and do you detect a sinister note with a clear reference to power through the word "master"? Does this resonate with the White House spokesperson presenting "alternate facts"? Humpty's message is clear, and, I suggest, as well understood by political leaders like Big Brother in Orwell's fiction as it is by political leaders in current times. Words can be used as a source of power, for good or ill, and in complex and confusing times they can define what people perceive as reality.

Let's pause and home in on that. The examples just presented demonstrate the power of words to make meaning. How much difference do you see between Winston Smith's work in Orwell's Department of Truth and the claims made by the President of the United States and his spokesperson? And if "facts" can now be "alternate" and personalised through the term "my truth" as they were in 2024 by the president of Harvard University, what exactly is a "fact"? Well, here's the thing: in the age of ambiguity, the successful manipulation of language relies on the assumption that concepts like "truth", "facts" and "real" are subjective. Then the words can indeed mean whatever someone wants them to mean, just as Humpty Dumpty asserted to Alice. It's well understood that people can innocently interpret words differently from what the conveyor of those words intended (e.g., Mackay, 1994). Combine that universal human trait with the kind of deliberate manipulation of language by powerful people, and we are indeed in a world of ambiguity.

Words can indeed be used as a source of power, for good or ill, and that has important implications for school leaders, as the use of words to make particular meaning is now an important capability for leadership. When there are competing interpretations of an event, an idea or a decision, people will receive different messages and make different meaning from them. There are times when school leaders need to convey an unambiguous "truth", even though we're living and working in the age of ambiguity. So what are the implications of this for decision-making?

Words and the management of meaning

As educational leaders, we don't have the luxury of resorting to "alternate facts" or "my truth" when making important decisions and communicating those decisions. Even though we're aware that people are likely holding differing "truths" in their minds – and asserting their right to hold them – parents, students and staff still look to the school leadership to make sense for them of what's happening, and they will not respect ambiguity. They are hoping for deeper meaning that they can believe in, and for wisdom and compassion in our work with their children.

This means it's now imperative for educational leaders to be *managers of meaning* (Limerick et al., 1998), and that this applies particularly to their decision-making: how they work through the process and how they then communicate their decisions. The words they use must mean the same thing to the decision-makers, who then have to ensure that those words mean the same thing when communicated to their communities. A good decision can still go wrong because of its wording or the way it's communicated or followed up, or because it's interpreted differently by different people.

This is especially difficult for school leaders, because people, especially parents, often have differing expectations about the purpose of schools. They hold different understandings – what Tom Sergiovanni calls *mindscapes* – about "why we are here". That means school leaders need to ensure that the school has agreed understandings of what is meant by words they use pretty much every day – words like "teaching", "learning" and "curriculum", and even words like "leadership". In your organisation does leadership mean "Follow me", "Do as I say", "What do we think of this idea?" or "Come with me" or any number of other meanings? Above all, the school community needs to have an agreed answer to the age-old question, *Why are we here?* with words like those in the previous sentence having similar meaning for everyone. That means understanding the implications of Sergiovanni's and Kahneman's assertions: people understand words – and by extension the world – in different ways. Humpty Dumpty was right, so it's important to take the time to define key words, and work with people to make sure that those words mean what you intend them to mean, both in making decisions and in communicating them.

> ... it's important to take the time to define key words, and work with people to make sure that those words mean what you intend them to mean, both in making decisions and in communicating them.

In essence, opinion and fact can become interchangeable in the age of ambiguity, as can lies and truth. The management of meaning is open to cynicism and dishonesty as well as being used for good. In making and communicating your decisions, you should choose your words with careful and deliberate integrity. The presenting of "alternate facts" and "my truth" is now commonplace, and people have become suspicious about the ways those in leadership positions often manipulate words. As we've seen, this doesn't just happen in authoritarian dictatorships. It's important to ensure that your management of meaning is not only done with care and integrity, but is also seen to be so.

Stay with this theme now. We're weaving our way through what all this means for school communities and education systems, and the decision-making processes of those who would lead them.

Reality and "reality"

"Reality never stands still for long." - Peter Drucker (2006, p. 47)

The journey through time we've been taking makes clear that physical and, especially, psychological change and disruption are not recent: changing perceptions of reality and truth have been evolving since at least the latter half of the 18th century, and not just in western societies. At the same time, you'll have noted the exponential increase in speed and intensity of those changes over the years, and the extent to which they are impacting on leadership.

School leaders simply must take this uncertainty, ambivalence and complexity into account in their work. Much of decision-making is now about managing meaning, and for those hoping for the pace of change to slow down and for everything to settle, I fear it will be like Samuel Beckett's two characters standing around waiting for Godot. And if you check in with

Mr Beckett today, I think you'll find that they're still waiting, while the world passes them by.

Grand narratives and "the spectre of meaninglessness"

In attempting to make sense of where we have arrived at today, Douglas Murray offers a big-picture explanation for the changes that have occurred over the 250 years we have just traversed:

> The simple fact [is] that we have been living through a period of more than a quarter of a century in which all our grand narratives have collapsed. One by one the narratives we had were refuted, became unpopular to defend or impossible to sustain. The explanation for our existence that used to be provided by religion went first, falling away from the nineteenth century onwards. Then over the last century the secular hopes held out by all political ideologies began to follow in religion's wake.
>
> In the latter part of the twentieth century we entered the post-modern era. An era ... defined by its suspicion of all grand narratives. However, as all schoolchildren know, nature abhors a vacuum, and into the post-modern vacuum ideas began to creep, with the intention of providing explanations and meanings of their own. (Murray, 2019, p. 1)

Murray goes beyond the continuing and increasing pace of change referred to by Toffler, Gleick and Fullan, suggesting that contesting ideas of what constitutes reality and truth have now penetrated deeply in western societies; and whether we like it or not, in our organisations and school communities the "grand narratives" he refers to are no longer sustaining us. To reprise Yeats's words:

> The falcon cannot hear the falconer;
> Things fall apart; the centre cannot hold

In an article published in January 2024, "Modern western malaise 500 years in the making", David De Carvalho draws on the words of Pope Benedict XVI in a 2007 encyclical, *Spe Salvi* ("Saved in hope"), where Benedict explores what he sees as the link between faith and hope, and suggests that without them we are destined to be "haunted by the spectre of meaninglessness". Powerful words, suggesting what happens when "the falcon cannot hear the falconer" and "the centre cannot hold". For a school, that is not a sustainable situation. Somehow, leaders need to make sense of this "meaninglessness" for their school communities: the falcon needs to be able to hear the falconer, and the centre needs to hold.

*

Peter Drucker's words above become more prescient as each year passes. Perhaps the greatest challenge of our time for educational leaders is to find within us the capacity and wisdom to make meaning out of the contested realms of truth and reality, both for ourselves and for our schools in their individual contexts, finding the words to create new narratives amid the constant push and pull by those who strive to present their versions as the "true" reality.

> *Perhaps the greatest challenge of our time for educational leaders is to find within us the capacity and wisdom to make meaning out of the contested realms of truth and reality, both for ourselves and for our schools in their individual contexts*

If we accept Peter Drucker's warning, that may well be the "reality" of leading and decision-making in schools in the age of ambiguity.

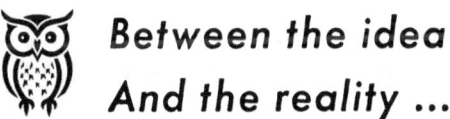

Between the idea
And the reality ...

- *We have drawn from the writings of novelists, poets, social researchers, organisational theorists, a philosopher, songwriters, musicians, a historian and a theologian, including two recipients of the Nobel Prize for Literature. Is there one (or more) of the writings you found yourself particularly relating to? Can you find your own words to explain why they resonate with you?*

CHAPTER 6
The way it is

> "He gave the 'I Have a Dream' speech, not the 'I Have a Plan' speech".
> – Simon Sinek on Martin Luther King Jr

Before you descend into despondency about how hard this is, it's important to consider some more perspectives on the 250 years we've been traversing through to the present. Australian social researcher Hugh Mackay maintains that change and uncertainty can actually be good for us, and are even necessary for our continuing development:

> ... To stay sharp, we need things to happen. We need unexpected events to crash into our lives and disturb our complacency; we need surprises; we even need emergencies if we are to be fully functioning, mature and balanced adults. Learning to deal with the hard stuff ... teaches us far more about ourselves than we can ever learn from breezing through the easy stuff. (Mackay, 2010, pp. 252, 255)

Learning to deal with the hard stuff ... teaches us far more about ourselves than we can ever learn from breezing through the easy stuff.

Peter Block is another who eschews a pessimistic view of our times and expresses optimism and hope if we're prepared to work on it. Block maintains that the positive power of community is the key to organisational and societal sustainability. Within that, he suggests, we can come to terms with uncertainty, and not fear it, but embrace it:

> We want desperately to take uncertainty out of the future. But when we take uncertainty out, it is no longer the future. It is the present projected forward. Nothing can come from the desire for a predictable tomorrow. The only way to make tomorrow predictable is to make it just like today. In fact, what distinguishes the future is its unpredictability and mystery. (Block, 2008, p. 105)

Those narratives struggle to find their way through the many gloomy offerings we are presented with about life today, and about the future. Mackay and Block are highly respected in their fields, and both assert that we need to maintain a sense of balance as we engage with the complexity, uncertainty, and indeed, mystery that all leaders have to work with today when making decisions. It's not just a negative agenda: it might be challenging, but it can also be good for us!

Metaphors, mindscapes, mental models and mindframes

The further good news is that amid the uncertainty and complexity, we've established that there are also things that hang together. The writings in Chapter 3 suggest that from right back to 1770, and probably well before that, the forces that have led us into the age of ambiguity have been working away, gradually evolving through various iterations. Both Mackay and Block are suggesting that as leaders we need to understand that evolving process, accept it, even embrace it, and find ways to manage and make meaning from it for ourselves and for our school and system communities.

Leaders, writers and thinkers who have come before us over the years have grappled with this, but now there's a new challenge. A school principal can't simply say at a school assembly or parent evening, "Well, we're living in the age of ambiguity so nothing is real or true", and expect students or parents to have confidence in their leadership or have a sense of where the organisation is heading. We need to engage people in managing the meaning of "reality" and "truth" as they apply to the life of this school or system, at this time.

That involves combining a sense of imagination, optimism and hope with a sense of meaning and purpose about why we're here doing what we're doing, and what is behind the decisions we're making. And it needs to have a coherent narrative: a story that goes deeper than test results and sporting premierships, through language other than clichés and soulless bureaucratic jargon, to touch the heart as well as the head: the dream before the plan. It needs to be simple, but not simplistic, and we need to make sure we include the imagination and youthful optimism of the students.

"While you hold it you cannot get lost …"

Consider these words:

> **The Way It Is**
> There's a thread you follow. It goes among
> Things that change. But it doesn't change.
> People wonder about what you are pursuing.
> You have to explain about the thread.
>
> But it is hard for others to see.
> While you hold it you cannot get lost.
> Tragedies happen; people get hurt
> Or die; and you suffer and get old.
> Nothing you do can stop time's unfolding.
> You don't ever let go of the thread.
> (William Stafford, 1998)

When Yeats wrote "The falcon cannot hear the falconer" and "The centre cannot hold", those potent metaphors cut through to our emotions as well as our intellect, capturing the sense of incoherence that Yeats was seeing around him. In "The Way It Is", William Stafford offers the metaphor of a thread that holds things together in our minds, finding coherence amid apparent incoherence. Let's follow that idea now, starting with the words we use and the metaphors we create with them and hold in our heads as we engage in decision-making.

Metaphors and mindscapes

You'll note that I've used the word *community* to describe the people in the schools and education systems we lead. Community is one of a number of metaphors we can use to conceptualise a school. Metaphors are powerful. They can capture complexity that direct or technical language doesn't; they often tap into our values and beliefs, and they can inspire their own narratives. Community is not everyone's conceptualising of schools and education systems, and it's frequently challenged by people holding competing political, social or economic metaphors. And it's always been that way.

Thomas Sergiovanni explores this through a word of his own invention – *mindscapes* – and he relates the concept directly to decision-making by educational leaders:

> Mindscapes – the mental pictures in our heads about how the world works – are often tacitly held. They program what we believe counts, help create our realities, and provide a basis for our decisions. What we do makes sense if it matches our mindscapes. And different mindscapes represent different realities. What makes sense with one mindscape may not make sense with another. Different realities can lead people to behave quite differently. (Sergiovanni, 1992, p. 9)

> *What we do makes sense if it matches our mindscapes.*
> *And different mindscapes represent different realities.*

While Sergiovanni is writing specifically about schools, Peter Senge suggests that the same concept applies in all organisations. He uses the term *mental models*, but you'll quickly see that he's writing about the same thing as Sergiovanni, using similar language. Writing in the same year as Sergiovanni, Senge suggests that *mental models* are our:

> ... deeply held internal images about how the world works, images that limit us to familiar ways of thinking and acting. That is why the discipline of managing mental models – surfacing, testing, and improving our internal pictures of how the world works – promises to be a major breakthrough ...
>
> The problems with mental models arise when the models are tacit – when they exist below the level of awareness. (Senge, 1992, pp. 175-76)

In a later work, John Hattie and Klaus Zierer write about *mindframes* – their term for what teachers hold in their heads about why they do what they do – and make the point that this is where their decisions about what and how they teach emanate from:

> How we **think** about the impact of what we do is more important than **what** we do. (Hattie & Zierer, 2018)

Hattie and Zierer are drawing here from Simon Sinek. Sinek offers the words of Martin Luther King Jr as an example. Sinek suggests that while there were many leaders in the civil rights movement in the United States in the 1960s, it was King's thinking and in particular why he was saying what he said that inspired 250,000 people to turn up for the March on Washington in 1963 and to hear his speech on the steps of the Lincoln Memorial:

> He gave the "I have a Dream" speech, not the "I Have a Plan" speech. It was a statement of purpose, and not a comprehensive twelve-point plan to achieving civil rights in America. Dr King offered America a place to go, not a plan to follow. The plan had its place, but not on the steps of the Lincoln Memorial. (Sinek, 2009, p. 129)

You can choose the terminology of Sergiovanni, Senge, Sinek, or Hattie and Zierer, but the concepts of mindscapes, mental models or mindframes all emanate from the "why", and it is too powerful to ignore. From here on, I'll use "mindscapes" as my preferred word to represent the concept. I'm urging you to choose one of those three terms for yourself or find your own words to capture it, because those writers are essentially offering a significant learning: what we hold in our heads about our ways of seeing the world, and why we see it that way, directly influences the decisions we make, how we make them and what we do to act them out – the head, the heart and the hand – and it's important. We need to be clear in ourselves about our own mindscapes, because while we're making decisions they're constantly at work, whether we're aware of it or not.

Senge explains why not only identifying our own mental models but sharing them with colleagues is important:

> Because mental models are usually tacit, existing below the level of awareness, they are often untested and unexamined. They are generally invisible to us – until we look for them. (Senge, 2000, p. 67)

I urge you to look for them: to think deeply and creatively about your own mindscapes and to encourage your colleagues in leading your organisation, school or system to find the words that articulate theirs, and to share them with one another, constantly looking at "why", so with your team you can forge a common language and establish common ground in the ways you conceptualise your leadership, and indeed, how you conceptualise your school. That's because within your mindscapes lie the drivers of your decision-making. Every decision you make, every opinion you contribute to conversations with your leadership team, or with staff, students or parents, is emanating from those mindscapes. That's a good reason to be clear not only about what they are, but why you hold them.

*

Thirty years after Sergiovanni and Senge, Daniel Kahneman, Olivier Sibony and Cass Sunstein are surely talking about the same thing as Sergiovanni and Senge when they write about what they call "human judgement":

> Most of us, most of the time, live with the unquestioned belief that the world looks as it does because that's the way it is ... We rarely question those beliefs ... We can live comfortably with colleagues without ever noticing that they actually do not see the world as we do. (Kahneman et al., 2021, p. 31)

That is a neat way to describe how mindscapes work, and it deepens our understanding of how "reality" and "truth" are dependent on how people see the world. Further, that the quote above comes 30 years after those of Sergiovanni and Senge is an important reminder that research from the past often remains relevant if it holds insight and wisdom for the present. Recency doesn't necessarily signify relevance or progress.

Why are we here?

Let's return to the *why*, as posed by Simon Sinek. In Ancient Athens, philosophers stood on street corners and engaged passers-by in conversations, asking questions like "What is happiness?" or "What is love?" One question they often asked was, "Why are we here?" Leaders need to ask that question today, and the thing is: each of us already holds the answer to that tacitly and perhaps unknowingly in our mindscapes: it's there in "the silence of the mind", waiting to be translated into words and shared when we opt to do so.

Let me reveal my response to *Why are we here?* as it relates to leadership. I believe Peter Block is right in affirming the positive power of community: so much so that *community* is my fundamental metaphor for schools. Call it my professional mindscape. It's my "reality" and my "truth" about schools and education. Communities care for one another; they share values and beliefs; they learn together, face adversity, and solve problems together; and they share a vision of what might be. After conscious and unconscious reflection about this over many years, this is my educational mindscape:

> Schools are places of human development. They are not factories; they are places of potential, not product.

That's why we're here. In my mindscapes, the purpose of schools is to nurture and build on the potential of every person, including the adults.

That's why – irrespective of external political or societal pressures, or legislative, system or regulatory requirements – *community* holds as my metaphor for schools. Underpinning all my decision-making within the world of education is the deep belief that this is why we are here. I urge you to discover for yourself and your organisation your answer to *Why are we here?* It will establish the *why* you're holding in your mindscapes; it's already there in "the silence of the mind", waiting for you to consciously engage it in your decision-making. Find the words to capture it and you're already on the way to a deeper understanding of why you do what you do. And when you've found the words, share them and invite colleagues to share theirs. As Senge suggests, having different mental models (mindscapes) from those you work with is only a problem when they remain tacit.

This presents a particular challenge for school leaders, as forging shared values, beliefs and norms in any community means bringing together people's different mindscapes and finding common ground. It takes vision, patience, empathy and relationship-building, along with a serious dose of meaning and wisdom. And it goes beyond standardised tests and exam results, an ATAR rank, and sporting premierships. Those can be important in the life of a school, but unless your mindscapes tell you so, they're not at the core of why you get out of bed in the morning and come to school.

*

So much for our mindscapes or mental models about schools and systems. If that isn't challenging enough, we have to accept that we can't shut out the external pressures that impinge on our organisations: accepting contested views of "reality" and "truth" means also understanding and accepting that schools are always reflective of their wider societies: whatever is out there in society will always find its way into our schools, sometimes in ways we didn't expect, and sometimes in ways we don't like.

> *... whatever is out there in society will always find its way into our schools, sometimes in ways we didn't expect, and sometimes in ways we don't like.*

That's what you face as a leader making decisions that affect your school community. As you work with teachers, support staff, students and parents, leading in the age of ambiguity is your responsibility. To your credit, you've stepped up where many are not prepared to go. It's a tough call, and I've learnt that to do it we must start by being clear about why we're here and understanding why those we work with are here. Your answer to that question reveals why you see the organisation you lead, and its context, in the way that you do.

If all this has you at a crossroads because you're unsure about what it means for where you are with your leadership and decision-making, perhaps you can take a hint from another poet:

> Two roads diverged in a wood, and I –
> I took the one less travelled by,
> And that has made all the difference.
> (Robert Frost, "The Road Not Taken")

 *Between the idea And the reality ...*

- *Are you prepared to dig deep in asking "Why are we here?" Can you find the words that capture your own mindscapes, mental models or mindframes? You can and you should, because then you'll have a deeper understanding about what lies beneath the surface when you're making decisions.*

- *When you've found the words, are you brave enough, confident and vulnerable enough, to share them with your colleagues, and even more widely with your school or system community? I'm willing to suggest that you'll find enough agreement there to indicate your leadership is in a good place.*

- *If you're at a crossroads, are you willing to reflect on Robert Frost's example? It just might make all the difference.*

CHAPTER 7

A roadmap or a compass?

"The dream is there, and it comes well before the plan."

Stephen Covey relates a well-known folk tale about a man sawing wood to prepare for winter. He's making heavy going of it, and the saw is clearly blunt. A friend drops by and suggests it would be easier if he paused and sharpened the saw. "I don't have time," the man replies. "Winter's coming and I've got to get it done quickly" (Covey, 2000).

Sharpening the saw: meaning, wisdom, and people

I'm a slow learner. I'd been a high school principal for several years before I realised that I didn't know enough about what I was doing. Like Sartre's nausea, it was a vague sense of uneasiness at first, hard to pin down, but I was sensing that amid the growing complexity of the work – especially in making decisions – I didn't have the necessary depth of understanding that I needed. Friends and colleagues told me that because I did a lot of professional reading and attended conferences and other professional learning opportunities I didn't need to undertake post-graduate study. Yet much of my thinking was intuitive – without a formal base – and it lacked coherence. While my leadership seemed mostly to be going well, that uneasiness wouldn't go away, and was in fact gradually increasing.

It prompted me to bite the bullet and enrol in post-graduate study, which I did through attending the Harvard International Summer Institute for School Leaders, then completing a Master's in Educational Leadership and Management with Professor Frank Crowther and his associates at the University of Southern Queensland. That took longer than I thought it would, and there were sacrifices, but the rewards were immeasurable for me, personally and professionally. After the very first reading of the course, the nausea quietly faded away.

Firstly, I found that much of my intuitive thinking was supported in research; but I also realised that my intuition is limited: some things are more important than I'd thought they were, others less so; my intuition was more reliable in some areas than others, and there were things that I had been unaware of beneath the surface, impacting on the issues I was addressing.

Secondly, there was an evolving coherence in the key findings of the research, and I found all of it relevant to my work, especially when making difficult decisions. Gradually there came a sense that I was finding some meaning amid complexity, and that I might even be developing some wisdom.

Thirdly, more than anything, I understood that the combination of my values, beliefs, experience, and learnings from research and now formal study was telling me that leadership, especially decision-making, is about more than systems, strategic plans, structures and policies. It is about those things, but I realised that at its core, leadership is about people, and it involves the head, the heart and the hand.

> *... at its core leadership is about people,*
> *and it involves the head, the heart and the hand.*

*

I'm confident you'll find that three words I've mentioned previously – *meaning*, *wisdom* and *people* – are key elements as you grapple with the kind of decision-making I faced in my work as a high school principal when working through difficult issues. They are there in the research for anyone who wants to look, but meaning, wisdom and people are often beneath the surface, and overlooked in much of the policy-making and media commentary today, especially regarding education. A focus on "outcomes" and superficial league tables often leaves the national and international educational leadership discourse out of balance, to the detriment of school leaders' ability to focus on what they and their teachers and most of their parents and students know they should be offering to the young people in their schools. And it goes beyond national and international standardised test results artificially fashioned into winners – and by default, losers.

*

Formal and informal research has become an integral element in my leadership, and without it I doubt that I'd have achieved much of substance as a principal. I still see school leaders who seem to think that their intuition, intelligence and charisma are all they need in their decision-making. Intuition and intellect are important – charisma less so – but I've learnt that they are not enough to lead in the age of ambiguity. It's why I'm offering this synthesis of my deepest learnings, inviting you to engage with it through your own mindscapes in your own context. And this is not coming to you from a guru. I'm a fellow traveller, and I've come to understand the insight behind Simon Sinek's statement quoted at the beginning of Chapter 6: even if you haven't yet uncovered it, the dream is there, and it comes well before the plan.

Rules, checklists ... and a compass

You're still reading, so you clearly sense that there's more to decision-making than composing policy documents and memorandums and pontificating at weekly assemblies. In the age of ambiguity, there are few rules or checklists for navigating, let alone leading, through this kind of terrain. You need a compass to guide you on where you want to go, and why, and from that you have to do the thinking that helps you compose the roadmaps that will guide you the way through. Other people's roadmaps won't necessarily help you, because their mindscapes are likely to be different from yours, as will their contexts, and what they see may not be what you see. You need to devise your own, personal roadmaps. Another simple concept, but again, far from simplistic.

> *... there's more to decision-making than composing policy documents and memorandums and pontificating at weekly assemblies.*

Six hours and 55 minutes

Abraham Lincoln: *If I had eight hours to chop down a tree, I'd spend six hours sharpening the axe.*

Albert Einstein: *If I had an hour to solve a problem, I'd spend 55 minutes thinking about the problem and 5 minutes thinking about the solution.*

You can see from their words that Lincoln and Einstein were emphasising the importance of taking the time to dig deep and do some serious thinking before moving to action – and they knew something about decision-making. Both emphasise the importance of the *thinking*: about positive initiatives, not just problems; about assets, not just deficits; looking for what is lurking beneath the surface, and regularly asking *why* we're doing this – all necessary for making decisions that will lead to effective solutions or initiatives that will strengthen your school or system.

It's the kind of thinking that takes time and focus, and it's not particularly fashionable in organisational leadership today, which may help to explain why so many school leaders are struggling. It's a kind of thinking that doesn't fit the decisive, action-oriented concept of leadership. Rather, it has a cumulative effect that calls on and nurtures three of those concepts I've mentioned earlier, which you also won't find much of in the national and international leadership discourse, but which are crucial to effective leadership today. Here they are again: *meaning, wisdom* and *people*.

It's a difficult, and if we're honest, daunting place to go. But as Hugh Mackay argues, it can also be exhilarating and rewarding. We know a lot about it now, and that's where we're going here. We're focusing on ways of thinking and conceptualising, and only then on solutions. The solutions will come for you in good time, in your unique context, if you can get the conceptualising and the thinking right; so for the busy, "time poor" leader, this is actually about efficient and effective use of your time. Get this right and you won't have to spend time cleaning up the mess that usually results from a decisive quick fix.

Now, back to the idea that on any journey, different people will see different things, and will therefore need different roadmaps to guide them. We're about to take a walk around a New York neighbourhood.

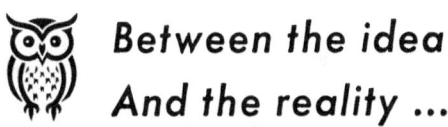

Between the idea
And the reality ...

- Do an audit on your current approach to your leadership work in your school. What proportion of your time would you say is transactional, and what proportion is transformational? Is there a message there for you?

- *Do another audit on how much of your decision-making is based on intuition, how much on emotion, how much on research, how much on experience, how much on your charisma – and think about how your mindscapes influence this breakdown. Is there a message there for you?*

CHAPTER 8
The management of meaning

"In this chaos, we will discover clarity." – Amanda Gorman

"… missing pretty much everything"

> You missed that. Right now, you are missing the vast majority of what is happening around you. You are missing the events unfolding in your body, in the distance, and right in front of you. (Horowitz, 2013, p. 1)

Alexandra Horowitz takes a daily walk with her dog around the blocks of her neighbourhood in New York City. One day she had a revelation:

> I had become a sleepwalker on the sidewalk. What I saw and attended to was exactly what I expected to see; what my dog showed me was that my attention invited along attention's companion: inattention to everything else. (2013, p. 2)

Having experienced this revelation, Horowitz decided to explore it further by taking a number of walks: first on her own, then with a number of people with differing backgrounds and interests. These included her 19-month-old son, a geologist, a specialist in lettering and calligraphy, an artist and illustrator, an etymologist, a wildlife scientist, an urban planner, a medical specialist, a blind person who traces the history of ornaments, and a sound designer for theatrical productions. After she'd completed those walks, she set off on her own to do the original walk around her neighbourhood again. With her new-found ways of looking for the things that were there but not immediately visible, she summed up: "As it turns out, I was missing pretty much everything".

Horowitz's reference to "attention's companion: inattention to everything else" elegantly captures perhaps the biggest trap that leaders can fall into when making decisions: seeing only what we expect to see; or worse, seeing only what we want to see.

Mistakes

In my years as a high school principal I was responsible for hundreds, probably thousands, of decisions. I think we made many good decisions, but we also made some mistakes. I say "we" because, though I was ultimately responsible, I rarely took a decision without checking in or deliberating with members of my leadership team and sometimes more widely. I learnt from bitter experience that I needed to do that.

On reflection, I think the mistakes were due to one or more of the following errors in judgement:

- We didn't have all the relevant information.
- We had all the information, but in moving quickly to a decision we missed something that was important.
- Sometime after we'd made the decision things occurred to us that we hadn't thought of at the time. We hadn't given time for reflection.
- We had all the information and we didn't miss anything, but there was something in there that was more important, or sometimes less important, than we realised it was.
- The issue affected people we didn't realise it affected. We needed their commitment to the decision, but we hadn't included them in our deliberations.
- We actually made the right decision, but we didn't communicate it clearly and effectively, including the reasoning behind the decision, especially to those it affected.
- Our follow-up to the decision wasn't strong enough or clear enough.

Perhaps you've picked up on the common theme in those mistakes: all of them happened because we missed things. Sometimes we had missed basic information or got communicating the decision wrong, but more often than not it was because we weren't able to fully understand the nuances and complexities that were all there in front of us. There were things we didn't see, even though they would have been visible to us if we'd known to look for them; and on some occasions we saw everything but there were some things whose significance we'd failed to understand, seeing it as simple when there was complexity. And of course, they were mistakes we didn't know we were making until later when the decisions came to grief. There has to be a better way.

*

Conventional wisdom suggests that leaders will always make mistakes and that we need to accept that, learn from them, and move on. True enough. But how easy is it to learn from a mistake when to the best of your ability you've covered all the bases, or when you've been confused or even immobilised by the sheer complexity of an issue? Unless we can find ways to think things through and analyse them at a deeper level, we'll continue to make the same mistakes; or worse still, go into avoidance mode and try to ignore the complexity and pretend that it's all quite simple. That would be a bigger mistake than any of those listed above, and the temptation to do it has led to the demise of more than a few school leaders over the years. You have to go there.

"Contemplating the whole"

Let's take a closer look now at complexity, nuance and uncertainty. In 1987 James Gleick wrote *Chaos*, expounding on the then new and revolutionary science of chaos theory. As explained by Gleick:

> The simplest systems are now seen to create extraordinarily difficult problems of predictability. Yet order arises spontaneously in these systems – chaos and order together ... In weather, for example, this translates into what is only half-jokingly known as the Butterfly Effect – the notion that a butterfly stirring the air today in Peking can transform storm systems next month in New York. (Gleick, 1988, pp. 7–8)

Since the early 1990s, Peter Senge has been working on the concept of *systems thinking*, offering insight into why we miss things that are important in addressing an issue or solving a problem. In the following passage, Senge clearly alludes to the butterfly effect as he explains systems thinking:

> A cloud masses, the sky darkens, leaves twist upward, and we know that it will rain. We also know that after the storm, the runoff will feed into groundwater miles away, and the sky will grow clear by tomorrow. All these events are distant in time and space, and yet they are all connected within the same pattern. Each has an influence on the rest, an influence that is usually hidden from view. You can only understand the system

> of a rainstorm by contemplating the whole, not any individual part of the pattern.
>
> Business and other human endeavours are also systems. They, too, are bound by invisible fabrics of interrelated actions, which often take years to fully play out their effects on each other. Since we are part of that lacework ourselves, it's doubly hard to see the whole pattern ... (Senge, 1992, pp. 6-7)

In a later work, Senge relates systems thinking directly to schools. He refers to the multiple events school leaders deal with each day, and the temptation to provide an immediate response. Senge suggests that these responses are rarely solutions; they're invariably "quick fixes". He elaborates:

> But there's a very real chance that each quick fix will do more harm than good in the long run. Moreover, reacting to each event quickly, and solving problems as quickly as they come up, helps develop a kind of "attention-deficit culture" in the school system.
>
> Moving rapidly from one issue to the next, people grow highly skilled at solving crises instead of looking for ways to prevent them. (Senge, 2000, pp. 77-78)

Contributing further to why we tend to move to quick fixes, Professor of International Health Hans Rosling suggests human nature makes us our own worst enemies in our decision-making:

> I think this is because human beings have a strong dramatic instinct toward binary thinking, a basic urge to divide things into two distinct groups, with nothing but an empty gap in between We love to dichotomise. Good versus bad. Heroes versus villains. My country versus the rest ... and we do it without thinking, all the time. (Rosling, 2018, p. 39)

We love to dichotomise. Good versus bad. Heroes versus villains. My country versus the rest ... and we do it without thinking, all the time.

"[W]e do it without thinking, all the time." With those words, Rosling has encapsulated my main message to you: in the age of ambiguity, we can't do decision-making, and therefore leadership, without thinking about it. And it's rarely simplistic, even if we desperately want it to be.

In the story of the rats of Hanoi in Chapter 2, we saw an example of how – without systems thinking – a quick, decisive and well-meaning solution by leaders can have unexpected and even disastrous consequences due to the "invisible fabrics of interrelated actions". Indeed, Jason Murphy sums up that story elegantly:

> This story has it all – a beautiful tango between administrative arrogance and human ingenuity that ends in disaster ... Whenever we create a new system we provide a pipeline for something quite unexpected to come along and bite us. (Murphy, 2019, p. 26)

Please note the key word: *system*. Those entities that connect to other entities form a system whose interconnectedness is invisible to us on the surface, but we need to be aware that it's there. Missing that interconnectedness was the reason for most of the mistakes I and my leadership team made in that list above.

*

We turn now to a different context but the same issue: a researcher's concern about what she sees as lack of systems thinking in government approaches to a global problem.

Chemotherapy to cure a head cold?

At the time of writing, perhaps the most contested – indeed polarising – "truth" or "reality" across the globe is that of climate change. It ranges between two poles: denial on the one hand, and apocalypse on the other. Keeping in mind learnings from Gleick and Senge about chaos theory and the need for systems thinking in decision-making, consider this excerpt from a national newspaper article in April 2022:

> Climate scientist Judith Curry argues ... that climate change has become a grand narrative: that there is only one thing we can do to prevent societal problems – stop burning fossil fuels. This grand narrative leads us to think that if we urgently stop burning fossil fuels, then these other problems also would be solved.
>
> She argues the complexity, uncertainty and ambiguity of the existing knowledge about climate change is being kept away from the policy and public debates ... leaving no space for imagining what our 21st century infrastructure could look like with new technologies and greater

resilience to extreme weather events, or even to deal with traditional environmental problems. (Curry in Lloyd, 2022)

Curry is clearly referencing chaos theory and systems thinking: opening up, not narrowing how the issue is conceptualised; and she is also invoking Abraham Lincoln and Albert Einstein's statements about the importance of thinking before quickly moving to solutions. And she specifically refers to "complexity", "uncertainty" and "ambiguity": all conditions that characterise the world today.

Is this resonating with your decision-making in your school? Are you pausing to explore how systems might be at work beneath what you're seeing on the surface? Take care: it's happening, and if you ignore it your solution may not be a solution, but a quick fix that makes things worse.

*

In *Leading Minds*, Howard Gardner looks at leadership through the frame of cognitive psychology. Using that paradigm, he comes up with 11 people whom he sees as highly effective leaders. It's not the kind of list you'd expect: it includes Eleanor Roosevelt (but not FDR), the anthropologist Margaret Mead, and J. Robert Oppenheimer, who led the Manhattan Project to develop the atom bomb in the early 1940s.

In analysing Oppenheimer's leadership, Gardner refers to:

> ... his ability to help physicists see the "bigger picture" – how one physics problem or domain related to another, how physics connected with other sciences, to other areas of knowledge, and to the world of personal choices.
>
> He represented the literate, inter-disciplinary individual, equally at home in the laboratories of the sciences, the ateliers of the arts, and the libraries of history and literature. (Gardner, 1995, p. 100)

Gardner is surely describing a systems thinker, and he relates this capability to the effectiveness of Oppenheimer's leadership of a diverse group of scientists, all with their own priorities and aspirations in the field.

There is an unmistakable theme to what Curry and Gardner are saying here about leadership and decision-making: I'm confident that Senge is right about the visible and invisible connections of everything, and how difficult it is to see the whole pattern; and Hans Rosling is right when he cautions about our "strong dramatic instinct" to grasp for a simplistic binary response to complexity and ambiguity: all likely to lead to another "rats of Hanoi" story.

We can either take systems thinking seriously, or ignore it in the interest of being decisive and moving quickly to solutions. Celebrated organisational writer Tom Peters, in *Thriving on Chaos* (1991), urges organisational leaders to do just this, and make decisions based on the formula "Ready, fire, aim". On rare occasions, that will be needed, but I'm suggesting that Peters is wrong on this one, and if anything, systems thinking is probably more relevant today than it has been in the past – and that's especially so not only for governments, but also for the decision-makers in schools and education systems.

In the three examples referenced above – the rats of Hanoi, climate change, and the Manhattan Project – an understanding of systems thinking is either absent or present. Senge's work was first published over 30 years ago, and is widely included in tertiary leadership and management courses. It is far from new; yet how deeply has it penetrated in challenging the "decisive, action-oriented" model of leadership, or the binary conceptualising of an issue, especially among politicians? What did Oppenheimer grasp about leadership and decision-making that others didn't, and still don't? I leave it with you to decide whether you think decision-makers, including yourself, are learning from the examples and the lessons of history that we've just been looking at. And we'll see soon whether the River Valley High team have their heads around it.

"The management of meaning"

How, then, can we ensure that our decision-making takes account of the milieu of "chaos and order together"? We can do a lot better than the French authorities did in Vietnam in 1890; and it's relatively simple, but unless it's a crisis situation, it's not as simplistic as "Ready, fire, aim". We need to be prepared to consciously work in the age of ambiguity, with the need for nuance in situations that often involve competing principles and aspirations as well as the merging – sometimes clashing – of emotion and intellect. Michael Fullan expresses this as a set of apparently competing principles that together make a coherent whole:

> The paradox of complexity is that it makes things exceedingly difficult, while the answer lies within its natural dynamics – dynamics which

can be designed and stimulated in the right direction, but can never be controlled. (Fullan, 1999, p. 3)

Decisions: right or wrong, black and white, or … ?

If we can't control complexity, and we can't avoid it because it's become a fundamental element in modern life, how do we make effective decisions in our schools and education systems? I'm suggesting that with evidence-based thinking and preparation and an understanding of systems thinking and our own mindscapes, we can do it, and do it well. I flagged it earlier, and we return now to what David Limerick, Bert Cunnington and Frank Crowther have called "the management of meaning". The authors assert that decision-making and leadership based on rational analysis is now not enough:

> The development of vision and mission and the communication of such symbolic processes demands that they be **managers of meaning**. The glue that holds the network organisation together is a common corporate culture, a shared world of meanings that allows independent, autonomous action to be focused and collaborative. (Limerick et al., 1998, p. 122)

It's another simple, but not simplistic, concept. The authors suggest that combining experience and research, and engaging in the kinds of thinking processes that are likely to guide you through complexity toward the best decisions possible, is about making meaning out of complexity, and being able to articulate and engage others in that meaning. And that means having a clear sense of purpose, and an understanding of the importance of human factors such as reciprocal trust in the culture.

More on that later, but first it's important to accept that owing to layers of nuance and internal competing values, some issues are going to result in decisions that may be neither right nor wrong but offer a way through that addresses the issue at hand, and that everyone can live with and commit to, even if some are disappointed. That places importance on listening, skilfully finding the words to frame the issue, and being able to explain the rationale for the decision. That is what the management of meaning looks like.

It's challenging, but Peter Drucker offers some reassurance and wisdom for decision-makers, and it's particularly pertinent when leaders are grappling with difficult issues like the one the River Valley team are addressing.

Drucker is managing meaning by helping us to define "reality" as it relates to making decisions:

> Decisions are made by people. People are fallible; at best their works do not last long. Even the best decision has a high probability of being wrong. Even the most effective one eventually becomes obsolete. (Drucker, 2006, p. 46)

While that can be unsettling because of its acceptance of uncertainty and the likelihood that not everyone will agree with the decision, it's also reassuring, because we are stepping up and defining "reality". In doing so, we are also cognisant of Hans Rosling's observation earlier: that we tend to dichotomise issues. We know that in the age of ambiguity a decision is rarely between right or wrong. It's often a messy brew, and school leaders need the wherewithal that will enable them to work confidently with ambivalence: that is, to work with confidence to find meaning and purpose amid complexity, for themselves and for their school community.

> *We know that in the age of ambiguity a decision is rarely between right or wrong.*

Strategic planning or strategic thinking?

In 1994 the *Harvard Business Review* published an article by Henry Mintzberg that was to become a classic in organisation theory and practice. In essence, Mintzberg argued that in leadership and management there is too much strategic planning, and not enough strategic thinking.

Mintzberg was lamenting the way leaders are increasingly being pressured to move quickly to find solutions to problems, or to devise strategic plans and action plans, without necessarily taking time to think through the complexities inherent in the issues involved. Mintzberg saw the prevailing concept of leadership being defined as quick thinking, decisive and action-oriented, at a time when the world was in fact becoming more difficult for leaders to navigate. He saw the complexity beneath the surface where others just saw the surface, but I think even he would be in awe of the complexity today's world presents to leaders in their decision-making: rapid change, uncertainty, competing values and ambivalence, all combining to tax even the most capable leader.

Taking time to think before taking action is still widely viewed as weakness in leadership, voiced in mantras like "Too much talk, not enough action", "Time is money", "Too many meetings", or the Nike slogan, "Just do it". We still find instances of an effective leader being described as someone who "gets things done". Even Elvis got in on the act: "A little less conversation, a little more action", recorded in the late 1960s, was revived as the theme song for the 2002 Football World Cup. Today, four decades after Mintzberg's article and several decades after that World Cup, many leaders and managers are still learning – often through bitter experience – that Mintzberg was right, and Elvis was wrong; though in fairness to Elvis, his context was a lot simpler than that facing school leaders today.

We conclude this chapter with a specific look at schools and education systems, contrasting their complex nature with that of other organisations, and relating that to decision-making by leaders.

Schools and complexity

At an Australian College of Educators' national conference in Sydney in 1987 – seven years before Mintzberg's article was published, and my first year as a high school principal – Australian education academic Hedley Beare gave a keynote address in which he suggested that schools have become society's most complex organisations. He made a convincing case, and it had a big impact on me. Beare's case for the greater complexity of schools in comparison with other organisations was well captured by Julie Kochanek nearly 20 years later. She points out that in contrast to other organisations in society and in industry, the goals of schooling are not commonly agreed across society: some parents prioritise academic achievement; others put the quality of the learning experiences before the formal results; others expect the school to promote their own values and beliefs; some want to see cultural diversity and acceptance of difference; some want to see sporting premierships; businesses expect students to be prepared for the workplace; while still others see the role of schools as producing good citizens. And today some parents expect the school to be responsible for what used to be parental responsibilities. Kochanek then suggests:

> While expectations vary, there is little open discussion or debate within communities about what should be the aims of schooling and how schools might accomplish this. (Kochanek, 2005, pp. 2–3)

Implied in Kochanek's statement are two questions that are easily answered for most organisations, but not so easily for schools:

(i) What is our "product"? National and international standardised test results? A tertiary entrance ranking? Entry to desired pathways after Year 12? Preparation for the workforce? Personal and social development of students? Sporting teams' success? The school's position on a media league table? Good citizens?

(ii) Who are our "clients": students? Parents? Industry? Governments? Society in general?

Answering those questions is a tough call, yet they're legitimate questions. They are part of that bigger question, of course: *Why are we here?* A first response to both questions might be "all of them", posing a further question as to whether some are more important than others. School leaders need the capability to engage with their communities to address that conundrum, and it relates directly to their decision-making. We are indeed engaged in the management of meaning.

"I'll see it when I believe it"

Karl Weick has contributed insight to the way many organisations, including schools and education systems, actually function, offering the concept of "loosely-coupled organisations". According to Weick, "loosely coupled" means that while the organisation is ostensibly an entity, within it are elements, both human and physical, that have their own entities, linked with the organisation but also having degrees of autonomy. Weick suggests that a loosely-coupled organisation cannot be controlled by the organisation's formal leadership, and neither should it be: the combination of a broad sense of purpose with creative and independent ways of pursuing that purpose are, according to Weick, a major strength of loosely-coupled organisations like schools, if led skilfully and wisely. That sounds very similar to Fullan's "dynamics which can be designed and stimulated in the right direction, but can never be controlled".

Without using the terms mindscapes, mental models, or mindframes Weick invokes them:

> The guiding principle is a reversal of the common assertion, "I'll believe it when I see it" and assumes an epistemology that asserts, "I'll see it when I believe it" ...

Organisations as loosely coupled systems may not have been seen before because nobody believed in them or could afford to believe in them. It is conceivable that preoccupation with rationalised, tidy, efficient, co-ordinated structures has blinded many practitioners as well as researchers to some of the attractive and unexpected properties of less rationalised and less tightly related clusters of events. (Weick, 1977, p. 3)

I'm suggesting to you that an understanding and appreciation of schools as loosely-coupled organisations is an important element in school leaders' decision-making processes, and in communicating their decisions. Within any organisation, especially a school, there is a wide variety of viewpoints, and these can be a significant strength in working through complex issues as long as the formal leadership is able to both acknowledge them and synthesise them in positive ways in the process. If that can be achieved, the greater the involvement of people, the more they are likely to support the final decision, and the more likely the decision is to be effective. It's difficult and demanding, but significant rewards await leaders prepared to dig deep and do the thinking.

And this is where Alexandra Horowitz's walk around the block with her dog has led us.

We return now to the meeting at River Valley High, addressing an issue that has many of the hallmarks of the age of ambiguity. We are well and truly engaged in the management of meaning.

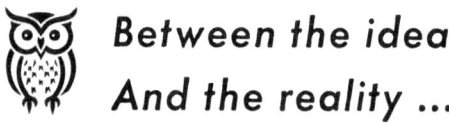

Between the idea
And the reality ...

- *Can you identify an event in the life of the school or system – a staff meeting, a parent meeting, a conversation about expectations of staff – where chaos theory and Senge's concept of systems thinking became evident? How did the way you handled it play out?*

- *No doubt you have a strategic plan in place. How closely did your design process follow Mintzberg's urgings about thinking before planning, Lincoln's sharpening of the axe, and Einstein's 55 minutes: 5 minutes formula?*

- *Stretch out with your colleagues on the ambiguity about the purpose of schools raised in this chapter. Are the two questions posed even the right questions for a school or education system? Whether they are or not, at some point you will need to have answers to these questions. They go to the heart of your leadership, and therefore to your decision-making.*
- *What is your take on Karl Weick's concept of loosely-coupled organisations and his claim that they can't be controlled? Can you apply the concept to your school or system by analysing it with your colleagues to see if you think Weick is correct?*
- *Do you own a dog? If so, take it on your next walk and see if you can experience something of Alexandra Horowitz's revelation by observing what your dog is interested in. (If you own a cat, don't try this.)*

CHAPTER 9
Competing principles

"Leave some wiggle room." – Maria Tostado

Emily's assignment, with its marijuana leaf standing out on the cover, sits on the table around which the team are seated. They are bemused. They haven't come across an issue like this one before, and they're finding it hard to separate their intellects and their emotions, leaving them unsure where to start.

Let's take a step back in time. Even though this particular incident had not been foreseen, in a sense the wording of the policy statement on illegal substances was part of the leadership team's preparation for dealing with it. The wording was influenced by Maria Tostado, principal of Garfield High School in East Los Angeles, whom the River Valley principal had met with while on study leave a few years earlier. They had discussed drug use by young people, and Maria had explained that Garfield High was deep in gang territory at that time and needed to make clear that while it cared for its students, it was also tough on drugs.

Garfield's leadership team had found that they needed to insert some flexibility into the wording of the policy statement, because in East Los Angeles things regularly came out of left field. Hence in the school's illegal substances policy statement the words "must expect to leave the school" were stated as the consequence of bringing an illegal substance onto the campus rather than "will be excluded from the school": just enough wiggle room to allow for the nuance of the current situation now facing the River Valley leadership team.

(At the time of writing, the Queensland state government was considering draft legislation that would make it legal for a person to carry a small amount of cannabis for private use. At the time of Emily's assignment cover, though, marijuana was not regarded as separate from other illegal drugs like LSD or cocaine. The penalties were serious, and there was strong feeling in the community against all illegal drugs. This was a serious issue for the school, involving its duty of care for Emily and the other students, its reputation, and state law.)

Drawing wisdom from the Garfield experience, the leadership team had done research and consulted with staff, parents and students to compose a three-part policy statement:

Illegal Substances

The River Valley High Illegal Substances Policy has three strands:

(i) *Educative:* The school commits to offering students factual, up-to-date education about legal and illegal drugs, free of any judgement about them.

(ii) *Health:* If a student, or a friend of a student, approaches an adult in the school for help because the student has got into difficulty with drugs, it will be treated as a health issue, and every possible support will be given to the student.

(iii) *Punitive:* Anyone in possession of an illegal substance at school, or who brings an illegal substance onto the school property, must expect to leave the school.

Maria Tostado had also explained that setting high expectations for academic achievement for the students, accompanied by support and encouragement to help them meet those expectations, was part of a trust-building process that the school felt was essential if they were to counter the youth drug culture of the district: a neat example of Senge's systems thinking, recognising the complexity of the issue and its interrelatedness with its surrounding community. The Garfield leadership team had also recognised the interrelatedness between students' wellbeing and their academic achievement, explained by Jay Mathews in his book about Jaime Escalante, the teacher who led the initiatives at Garfield. Twelve years after almost losing its accreditation, Garfield had more Advanced Placement Calculus students than all but three public schools in the country (Mathews, 1988).

The Garfield leadership's understanding about systems thinking – that student behaviour, wellbeing and academic achievement are linked and bound up in a bigger "system" – was clearly present in the mindscapes of Garfield's leadership when they devised their policy statement on illegal drugs. And informed by Garfield's example, so it was with the River Valley policy statement.

*

While the final decision will ultimately be the formal responsibility of the principal, the extended problem-solving team includes two non-educators: the business manager and counsellor. This is partly to help ensure that they have all the relevant information; but there is a further reason, again drawn from their research.

The reason for the composition of the group dates back to a discussion the members of the leadership team had some time back, based on the work of James Surowiecki. In *The Wisdom of Crowds*, Surowiecki puts forward compelling real-life examples to assert that even in complex situations the best decisions come when non-experts in the field are included in the deliberations. Surowiecki states:

> Under the right circumstances, groups are remarkably intelligent, and are often smarter than the smartest people in them. (Surowiecki, 2004, pp. xiii–xiv).

The leadership team were impressed with the factual examples provided by Surowiecki, some going back a long way historically, that lend credibility to his claim. Like Fullan's paradox earlier, it seems counter-intuitive, but Surowiecki bases his case – and the title of his book – on a concept we have already singled out, and will continue to: *wisdom*. The leadership team acknowledge Surowiecki's insights, and have been organising problem-solving groups at the school this way for some years when deliberating on complex issues.

*

When the team reconvene, Emily's class wellbeing teacher explains that Emily has told her friends that she was going to do this, so it's already big news among the students, and will soon be big news among the parents and the wider community, all watching to see how the school will handle it.

The leadership team have already made the decision that Emily will be sent home and the principal will phone her mother, a lone parent, explaining the situation and asking her to keep Emily home for the next few days and work with the school toward a solution. She is distressed but understands the difficulty of the situation. While at home, Emily is to think about the implications of bringing that substance onto the school campus and to write about it, including showing an understanding of the legal position she has placed herself and the school in.

The group ranges across possible ways forward. The further they go, the more complex and problematic it gets. The first question they always ask when confronting a difficult problem is: "Do we do something or do nothing?" They are aware of the research showing that sometimes it's actually best to do nothing, and to let the matter play out in its own time. Is this such a situation?

They quickly agree that to do nothing would invite the rumour mill and "Chinese whispers" to kick in even more than is already happening. They have a clear understanding of systems thinking, and they know that their decision will have a wide impact in the school community, some of it in ways they can't predict. They need to do something.

The principal suggests they identify the underlying issues involved here. The conversation evolves in a semi-structured way, presenting various lines of thought:

- Technically, this isn't about illegal drug use, dealing or supplying. Emily hasn't engaged in any of these, and she's been quite open in what she's done. At the same time, she's brought an illegal substance onto the school property in contravention of the school's policy on possession of illegal drugs.
- Emily's wellbeing has to be part of this, but she has to show some understanding and take some responsibility for the implications of her decision. She can't just walk away from this.
- Rules are rules and the policy statement is clear. She's broken the rules and she's broken the law.
- The three-part policy statement was carefully designed and worded. It's there to ensure students have an understanding about drugs and the laws that relate to them, aiming to have students make wise decisions when they come into contact with the drug culture, as they surely will.
- It's about more than Emily. One option is to make her an example of what happens if you bring drugs to River Valley High, and expel her. One student suffers but it's for the benefit of the rest of the students, and for the school's reputation in the wider community. It's "tough love".
- Are we prepared to live with using Emily as a scapegoat to give a strong message to the students and the community about illegal drugs at the school?

- If we treat it as a minor infringement of the school rules and counsel her on what she hasn't understood about this, we'll show that the school cares about its students and accepts that young people will make mistakes.
- If we treat it as a minor infringement and counsel her on what she hasn't understood about this, we'll give the impression that River Valley High is soft on drugs, leading to bigger problems in the future.
- It's important to show that River Valley High doesn't have a "drug problem".
- It's pure marijuana, so it can't be smoked or ingested in its current state. Is that relevant?
- Our decision is not going to please everybody.
- How we communicate the decision and follow it up is going to be important.

During the day some teachers drop in on members of the leadership team and offer thoughts and advice, which pretty much range across what the group has identified above.

Four principles soon work their way to the surface, potentially in competition with one another. Firstly, the school has a responsibility for Emily's wellbeing, and that includes how this matter is handled. Secondly, the school also has a responsibility to protect its students from the scourge of illegal drugs while they are at school. Thirdly, the school's reputation has to be protected. And fourthly, there is the state law on possession of illegal drugs.

This issue has the potential to divide the school community, so not only is the decision-making process complicated, but the way the decision is communicated to staff, parents and students will need to be done skilfully. The team are now deeply engaged in the management of meaning.

They meet again after school and stretch out further on the issues involved. It becomes clear that the mix of intellectual and emotional perspectives is troubling everyone, with all agonising over where this might lead. Everyone likes Emily and they don't want to discourage her feistiness. They accept that despite her provocative action she meant no harm. There isn't going to be a straightforward "right" or "wrong" response to this.

After close to two hours, the principal compliments everyone on their input and suggests they wrap up and sleep on it. There is clearly anxiety in the room, and one of the teachers suggests that by delaying their decision they might be deliberately avoiding taking action: that time is of the essence because the rumour mill is already at work, and they need to be decisive. Others are unwilling to make a decision at this stage, including the principal. They agree to "sleep on it" and meet early next morning.

Over a few years, the principal has cultivated a relationship with the district police, who have been invited to the school on a number of occasions to advise staff or students on various issues. He decides to address the legal situation by phoning and speaking with the senior officer. He asks for advice on a "hypothetical" situation that the school might face in the future. The police officer probably knows it's real, and he expresses confidence in the school's ability to handle the situation "if it were to occur". He explains that the police are dealing with many major issues and they would have confidence in the school handling it. That's one of the four principles dealt with: three to go.

*

The complexity, nuance, anxiety and ambivalence at work here will take some heroic thinking-through to reach a solution that is both ethical and practical, and to have their decision widely accepted by the school community. Indeed, sooner or later they will arrive at the philosophical question we have identified as at the core of decision-making: *Why are we here?*

But first, why "sleep on it"? Because they are tired? Because they don't think they can make further headway today? Because their brains are fuddled after all that thinking? Yes to all that; but the idea of "sleeping on it" has genuine substance, and we're about to embark on another thinking expedition to explore it.

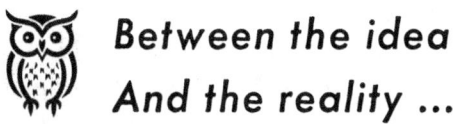

Between the idea And the reality ...

- *What do you think about the wording of the River Valley drugs policy?*
- *How well do you think the problem-solving team has conceptualised the issue in the dot points? Have they missed anything?*

CHAPTER 10

Who won the race?

"To be still and to wait" – Miriam-Rose Ungunmerr-Baumann

"Sounds of the deep"

We leave the River Valley group for now while they "sleep on it", and head to the Daly River in Australia's Northern Territory to visit an Aboriginal elder and reflect on a local cultural tradition.

Some years ago I was asked to work in the Northern Territory with young Aboriginal assistant teachers from remote communities and engage with them in leadership work. I was guided and assisted by an elder from the Daly River, Miriam-Rose Ungunmerr-Baumann. The evening before we began, I asked Miriam for her advice on how I should approach the week. I'd done a lot of preparation, most of it geared at engaging the group, but I was still keen to connect with them by drawing on their own cultural understandings about leadership, of which I knew little.

Over a cup of tea, I asked Miriam what the group might be expecting from me. She said, "Norm, at the moment you're just another white fella who's going to come here and tell us what we should be doing. Then you'll fly out and nothing will change." I told her that's exactly what I was concerned about, and asked her advice on how I might be able to connect with the group and engage them. She assured me she'd help with that, and she did, with insight and empathy. We had an uplifting week with the young assistant teachers, ranging through their own community situations, Martin Luther King, the 1960s soul band Booker T and the MGs (two white members, two African-American, including the band leader), Vincent Lingiari and the Wave Hill land rights campaign (including Paul Kelly's song "From Little Things Big Things Grow", which became a theme for the sessions), to Nelson Mandela. When we wrapped up on the Friday, the group presented me with a book of Indigenous stories from around the Territory. At the front they'd written some personal messages. Miriam had written: "Dear Norm – For a white fella you're a fast learner". It's probably my most treasured compliment.

*

The link with decision-making comes in here. Miriam and I had some wide-ranging conversations that week over more than one cup of tea. At one point she told me about the Daly River people's concept of *dadirri*, and gave me a copy of what she'd written about it. She begins:

> Ngangikurungkurr is the name of my tribe. The word can be broken up into three parts: ngangi means word or sound, kuri means water, and kurr means deep. So the name of my people means "the Deep Water Sounds" or "Sounds of the Deep".
>
> This reflection is about tapping into that deep spring that is within us ... It is something like what you would call "contemplation".
>
> Many Australians understand that Aboriginal people have a special respect for Nature. ... What I want to talk about is another special quality of my people. I believe it is the most important. It is our most unique gift. It is perhaps the greatest gift we can give to our fellow Australians. In our language this quality is called **dadirri**. It is inner, deep listening and quiet, still awareness.
>
> Dadirri recognises the deep spring that is inside us. We call on it, and it calls on us.

> *Dadirri recognises the deep spring that is inside us.*
> *We call on it, and it calls on us.*

> There is no need to reflect too much and to do a lot of thinking. It is just being aware. ...
>
> Our Aboriginal culture has taught us to be still and to wait. We do not try to hurry things up. We let them follow their natural course – like the seasons. We watch the moon in each of its phases. We wait for the rain to fill our rivers and water the thirsty earth ... (Miriam-Rose Ungunmerr-Baumann, 1988)

When you read those words, you might understand why the concept of *dadirri* has had a lasting impact on me, including on my approach to leadership, and decision-making in particular. There is a cultural uniqueness here that cannot be fully comprehended by a non-Aboriginal mind, but the idea of a "deep spring that is within us", flowing quite apart from words and conscious thinking, has some resonance with the western concept of the subconscious, and the importance of letting it do its work quite apart from our conscious mind. As in "sleeping on it".

(A few years later, in 2021, Miriam would be named Senior Australian of the Year.)

"Slow knowing"

While *dadirri* is a uniquely Aboriginal concept, Miriam's reference to "deep listening and quiet" recalls Daniel Kahneman's words in Chapter 3: "The mental work that produces impressions, intuitions and leads to decisions goes on in silence in our mind". That "silence in our mind" is what we are discussing here, and we move now to the work of Guy Claxton, who has researched and written widely on cognitive science. In elaborating on the concept he calls "slow knowing", Claxton challenges the "quick thinking/decisive leadership model" discussed earlier:

> In pre-seventeenth century Europe a leisurely approach to thinking was much more common, and in other cultures it still is … However, the idea that time is plentiful is in many parts of the world now seen as laughably old-fashioned and self-indulgent … Within the Western mindset, time becomes a commodity, and one inevitable consequence is the urge to "think faster": to solve problems and make decisions quickly … the faster problems are solved, the better. (Claxton, 1997, pp. 4–5)

Claxton goes back to Ancient Greece to tap into some timeless wisdom. For anyone growing up in western society, a mention of the story of the tortoise and the hare is likely to bring instant recognition about a race, and who won the race. We know that Aesop wrote that story and others with animal characters, not for children but for adults. The animals all have human qualities, and the stories range across social, political, religious and ethical themes. The stories are guides to human behaviour, and their longevity suggests that as well as being entertaining, they are fables with enduring sources of meaning and wisdom.

In *Hare Brain, Tortoise Mind* (1997), Claxton uses Aesop's race between the hare and the tortoise as a metaphor to explore our conscious mind, which acts in the immediate present and tends to jump around in a largely undisciplined way with a sense of urgency, in contrast with what he calls our "tortoise mind": our subconscious, which moves slowly at its own pace, processing information irrespective of what is happening around it, even working while we sleep. He points out that the hare is quick-thinking, confident and decisive – the "hare brain" – while the tortoise is ponderous and apparently slow-thinking – the "tortoise mind". As we engage in decision-making, Claxton suggests that the hare brain and tortoise mind are conducting a version of that race in our heads, with the hare brain pressing us to hurry up and make a decision, and the tortoise mind urging us to slow down and let our thoughts percolate.

Claxton offers growing scientific evidence that "the more patient, less deliberate modes of mind are particularly suited to making sense of situations that are intricate, shadowy or ill-defined". That sounds like situations that are likely to face leaders making decisions in the age of ambiguity. And I'm sure you've already noticed how resonant Claxton's thinking is with *dadirri*, which also reaches back in time for its source.

Ungunmerr-Baumann again:

> When I experience dadirri, I am made whole again. I can sit on the riverbank or walk through the trees; even if someone close to me has passed away, I can find my peace in this silent awareness. There is no need for words.

Dadirri and slow thinking might seem a long way from the decision-making process taking place at River Valley High, but Ungunmerr-Baumann and Claxton are surely talking about the management of meaning: something complex needs time if it's to be understood and a wise decision made and communicated. It's simple but far from simplistic. In essence, a timeless Australian Indigenous concept, a fable from Ancient Greece, and recent thinking by a British scientific researcher come together, pointing to the importance for school leaders of what Claxton calls "slow knowing". He states that, based on extensive research, it's clear that if given time, slow knowing can work in the human mind in ways that enable us to conceptualise

> ... patterns of a degree of subtlety which normal consciousness cannot even see; make sense out of situations that are too complex to analyse; and get to the bottom of certain difficult issues much more successfully than the questing intellect. They will detect and respond to meanings, in poetry and art, as well as in relationships, that cannot be clearly articulated. (Claxton, 1997, p. 4)

We will return to River Valley in good time, but first we need to consolidate this thinking expedition and make meaning from it. I'm suggesting that the special constellation of cross-cultural wisdom expressed as *dadirri*, the "silence in our mind", the hare and the tortoise, and "slow thinking", is a gift resting just below the surface, waiting for school leaders to find it and hold it close.

You will find it if you look for it, and Ungunmerr-Baumann, Kahneman, Aesop and Claxton offer compelling reasons for allowing time to do just that. I'm suggesting that school leaders whose decision-making processes discount the underlying power and potential significance of "sleeping on it" are missing something of significance, and if they miss it, their decisions may well have as much success as Aesop's hare.

*

Has this historical and cultural interlude got you thinking about your own decision-making in your school or system? Like Alexandra Horowitz in the previous chapter, be patient now, and tune your antennae to what you might be missing, because it's there even if you're not seeing it yet. We are still on a thinking expedition, and continuing to walk the long and winding road that will ultimately lead us back to that meeting at River Valley High.

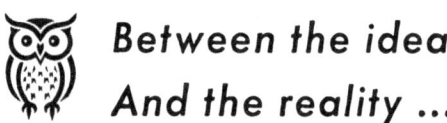

- *Ernest Hemingway wrote: "After writing a story I was sure this was a very good story, although I truly would not know how good until I read it over the next day" (1959, p. 14).*
- *Reflect on the concepts of* dadirri, *the "silence in our mind", and "slow thinking", as they relate to your current decision-making processes, and engage your colleagues in conversation about them. Is there something here to take with you on your leadership journey?*

CHAPTER II
What we can't see

> "Between the idea
> And the reality ...
> Falls the shadow."
> – T. S. Eliot

What's in there?

A few years ago I was privileged to visit the Rijksmuseum in Amsterdam, taking in the beauty and subtlety of the Dutch masters of the 17th century. As I moved around, I found myself drawn to the paintings of Pieter de Hooch, whose work I hadn't encountered before.

What initially drew me to him was a strange sense of incompleteness, even though the paintings were clearly completed. "Mother and Child in an Interior" is an example. The painting is true to its title, depicting a mother and her child in a room. But when you pause and look more closely, your eyes are naturally drawn beyond them. De Hooch has used light, shade and perspective to move our interest to the background, where we look through an open door to a partial view of a room. There is a chair, and on the wall a portrait. Further in, there is an open window, and through it we can glimpse what may be a courtyard or a street or laneway.

There's mystery here, and the beguiling sense of something important but not visible to the viewer. Who sits on that chair? Who is the subject of the portrait on the wall? (It's deliberately vaguely drawn.) Is there anyone else in the room? And what is outside the window? There's something there, but we can't see it from where we're looking – just like a school leader confronted with a complex issue.

What's implied here? If we look from a different angle, will we be able to see the whole picture? Hold on to those questions.

The power of culture

We leave Amsterdam now and head across the Atlantic to a village in Peru.

In his classic work on change theory, Everett Rogers (2003) relates the story of a two-year intensive campaign by health officials in Peru, who were attempting to solve a problem with the health of people living in a village in the foothills of the Andes.

Villagers were presenting at the local clinic with diseases like typhoid and dysentery. They were treated, they recovered, then the same people returned later to be treated for the same diseases. After investigation by health officials from the city, the cause of the problem became clear: the people were drinking from a local creek containing the bacteria that cause the diseases. The solution was simple: the villagers needed to boil their drinking water to kill the bacteria.

Health officers, including a doctor, visited every home in the village, teaching the families about germs, how bacteria in the drinking water were causing the illnesses, and that all they needed to do was boil the water before drinking it. That simple act would pretty much eliminate disease from the village. Two years later, however, the villagers were still locked in the cycle of illness, treatment, recovery and recurring illness. What had gone wrong?

The answer lay hidden between the idea and the reality. Unknown to the officials, beneath the surface was a local cultural belief about "hot" and "cold". Rogers explains that according to this belief, all liquid and solid foods, including medicines, are inherently "hot" or "cold", where cold equates to "good" and hot to "bad". This manifests itself across village life in areas such as food, health, pregnancies, education and child-rearing. Village children learn it from an early age. So where does that place boiling water?

On the surface, the issue was similar to the rats in the sewers of Hanoi: a basic scientific case of cause and effect. At a deeper level, though, lay a cultural belief supported by a logic that overrode any scientific understanding of germ theory. This was not known and understood by the health workers, none of whom were familiar with the local culture. They had quickly discovered the scientific dimension of the problem, but in their decision-making they overlooked the cultural perspective. It was there, but they weren't looking for it, so they didn't see it.

Pieter de Hooch uses visual art to create a sense of something important but incomplete and mysterious. The viewers know it's there, but they are unable to see it from where they're looking. In the lines from "The Hollow Men" quoted earlier, T. S. Eliot uses words to suggest something similar, with the metaphor of a shadow hiding the mystery of what is there between the idea and the reality. If we want to turn an idea into reality, suggests Eliot, we need to go into the shadow and shed light on it.

Metaphorically, if the health workers in Peru had been able to see into de Hooch's hidden rooms, or bring light into Eliot's shadow, they might have realised that they were dealing with the complexity and nuance of village culture, not just a scientific concept. That might not have fully solved the problem, because they might not have realised that the cultural belief was stronger than the scientific truth. Nevertheless, they would have been thinking and working in the deeper realm beneath the surface, giving them a greater possibility of engaging the villagers in enacting a solution.

*

By now you'll have realised why we've taken the words of an American poet, viewed a painting by a Dutch master, and visited a village in Peru. It's a way of demonstrating the power of culture to dominate systems and structures, even at times overriding basic science and logic. It's a theme we'll return to, expressed with some bluntness in words attributed to Peter Drucker:

> Culture eats strategy for breakfast.

It's not that structures, systems and strategy aren't important. They are. It's just that if there is a tension or a clash between proposed systems or structures and the prevailing culture, it's culture that will almost always win out; a strategic or structural solution may not be a solution at all. And research about organisations, including schools, makes clear that cultural changes are more complex and therefore much harder to accomplish than structural ones, and they take longer to work through. Former Lord Mayor of Melbourne and Australian industry leader Ivan Deveson (1997) offers a further dimension:

> The culture of an organisation can be stronger than an individual manager's values. (p. 114)

If Deveson is right – and my experience tells me he is – then understanding culture is especially relevant for school leaders. And if Hedley Beare and Julie Kochanek are right about schools being society's most complex organisations – and I think they are – keep in mind that Beare made that observation in 1987 and Kochanek in 1995, before the age of social media, and before today's identity politics and the related ways of thinking about reality and truth that now pervade the age of ambiguity, and before the onset of artificial intelligence. If they were right then, they are probably more right today.

The same applies to what Abraham Lincoln, Albert Einstein and Henry Mintzberg were saying about the need for preparation and thinking before moving to strategies and solutions. It suggests that if leaders are to make effective decisions involving the human development of the young people and adults in their schools and systems, they will need to find ways to bring light into Eliot's shadow, see fully into de Hooch's partly-hidden room, and in doing so understand the power of organisational culture.

*

I hope this is hanging together for you. We're looking beyond what we can see on the surface, seeking different ways to see what might be concealed in the shadow of an idea, behind the half-open doors and windows of a room, or in the prevailing culture of a village or school, helping us to make sense and then manage meaning in one of the most complex roles in society today: educational leadership. Along the way we're drawing meaning and wisdom from such diverse sources as an elder from the Daly River, a British cognitive science researcher, a story-teller from Ancient Greece, an American poet who was awarded the Nobel Prize in Literature, a Dutch master from the 17th century, and a cultural artefact from the foothills of the Andes. We're covering a lot of territory as we walk this long and winding road, but stay the course: it all hangs together, and it's leading us to greater clarity and understanding about making decisions in the milieu of the age of ambiguity.

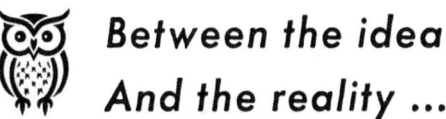
Between the idea
And the reality ...

- *How does your approach to strategic planning match up with Henry Mintzberg's claim about the difference between strategic planning and strategic thinking?*

- *When addressing a difficult issue, have you sometimes sensed that there is more there than you're seeing, but you're unable to identify what it is?*

- *Have you experienced or observed a situation where culture has proven to be more powerful than science, logic, structures, systems or strategies in addressing an issue or problem? If so, discuss it with colleagues and see if you can make some meaning from it.*

CHAPTER 12
Culture and structure

"Beneath the conscious awareness of everyday life in schools, there is a burbling rivulet of thought and activity. The underground flow of feelings and folkways wends its way, beckoning people, programs, and ideas toward often unstated purposes: This invisible, taken-for-granted flow of beliefs and assumptions gives meaning to what people say and do." – Terrence Deal and Kent Peterson

Importance and urgency

The River Valley leadership team has in the past grappled with the tension between perceptions of urgency on the one hand and importance on the other, as conceptualised by Stephen R. Covey in his four quadrants of time management (Covey, 1994). The team had determined that at times they were avoiding the "important but not urgent" quadrant in Covey's table, and as a result were neglecting an important area of their work. In his "important but not urgent" quadrant, Covey lists *preparation*, *values clarification*, *prevention*, *planning*, *relationship building*, *empowerment* and *true re-creation*. You'll have noticed that all of these lie mostly in the culture of the school – the human dimension – rather than in its systems and structures.

Several years ago, in response to this gap in their work, and with an increasing concern about their neglect of that area, the leadership team took the decision that irrespective of how busy they were, they would devote a full day each term to their own professional team learning, working away from the school. They would focus on stretching out on a big-picture issue in the life of the school, or on a concept one of them had encountered in an article or book, or at a conference. It may or may not have direct relevance to the life of the school at that time or lead directly to action on a current issue, but they believed it would deepen their understanding of their leadership work and would ultimately inform their decision-making.

Around the same time, the principal had begun a master's course in educational leadership and management. His exposure to the research and thinking about leadership, both historical and current, showed insights into some of the nuances and complexities of organisational behaviour that he and the other members of the leadership team had observed or intuited and had puzzled over, but not necessarily fully understood. Soon, topics from the course found their way into those big-picture sessions. In a sense, the leadership team had embarked on the master's course together.

Leadership: it's more than positional

We're taking a moment now to explore further the relationship between structure and culture in the school. When Emily's English teacher handed that assignment to the principal and said, "It's your problem now", in one sense that was true: according to the school's administrative structure, the principal's duty of care means he is legally responsible for everything that happens in the school. In another sense, though, it wasn't true. That teacher also accepted responsibility to join with the leadership team in addressing the issue, giving significant amounts of her time, as did the other two teachers and the counsellor, reflecting a fundamental element in River Valley's culture: that of shared leadership. But that doesn't just happen because a leader says it's happening. Come with me now on another thinking expedition and reflect on this challenge from Peter Block:

> We need ... to deglamorise leadership and consider it a quality that exists in all human beings. We need to simplify leadership and construct it so that it is infinitely and universally available. (Block, 2008, p. 85)

For some years, the leadership team had been influenced by the work of Frank Crowther and his colleagues at the University of Southern Queensland, extending and refining their understanding of shared leadership through what Crowther and his team have termed *parallel leadership*:

> Parallel leadership ... encourages a relatedness between teacher leaders and administration leaders that activates and sustains the knowledge-generating capacity of schools. Parallel leadership is a process whereby teacher leaders and their principals engage in collective action to build school capacity. It embodies mutual respect, shared purpose, and allows for individual expression. (Crowther et al., 2002, p. 38)

John MacBeath from Cambridge has also recognised this form of shared leadership. Using different language from Crowther, MacBeath suggests that while shared leadership is generally a good thing, genuine shared leadership is both *distributed* and *distributive* (MacBeath et al., 2003).

MacBeath defines *distributed* leadership as essentially top down, with the principal delegating positions of responsibility to chosen people. MacBeath suggests that while this is likely to enhance the quality of decision-making in the school, power stays at the top: it is essentially about structure, and depending on how the principal manages it, it can still be a "zero sum" version of power – a set amount of power is available in the school, and if some of it is shared with others there is less left with the principal (Covey, 1992).

At a deeper level, and more in keeping with Crowther's concept of parallel leadership, *distributive* leadership bubbles up from below. It's bottom up, and takes an "abundance" view of power in the school – there is an infinite amount of power, and the more power is shared within a defined framework, the more effective decision-making and therefore leadership in the school are likely to be (Covey, 1992). Most importantly, while distributed leadership is more about structure, distributive leadership is more about culture. Distributive leadership encourages initiatives from staff and overtly recognises this as leadership work, imparting leadership opportunities to everyone, not just those in formal leadership or management roles. When both are in place, there is a "top down/bottom up" dynamic in place, with the systems, structures and culture reinforcing one another. It is reflective of Karl Weick's "loosely coupled organisations", accepting that attempts at control won't work, but a culture of trust and respect and an abundance mentality will, if the leadership is skilled, enlightened and secure enough to invoke them within an agreed framework.

My point here is that parallel leadership and distributive leadership are generated in the culture of the school more than in its structures. Whatever happens through the structures needs to emanate from the culture, suggesting that defining and strengthening the culture and matching the infrastructure with it is really the key to successful leadership and decision-making in the school: ideally the structures will be designed to complement and support the culture.

> *... parallel leadership and distributive leadership are generated in the culture of the school more than in its structures.*

Let's pause here for a moment. *Abundance view, zero sum view, parallel leadership, distributed leadership, distributive leadership, trust, respect ...* are they just words? Do they have any real meaning in the life of your school or system? Do they give you cause to think about how power works, and its relevance to leadership and decision-making in the age of ambiguity? We are in the business of the management of meaning and developing wisdom: making sense of complexity, nuance and uncertainty, not just for ourselves but for our school communities. And the way we use words must go beyond speaking them.

So, shared leadership at River Valley means parallel leadership, incorporating distributed and distributive leadership, all embedded in the school culture. It's evidenced by teachers feeling confident, and some even seeing it as their responsibility, to drop in on members of the leadership team during the day to offer their thoughts and advice on the predicament Emily's marijuana leaf has presented.

If you're brave enough to take an abundance approach to leadership – and by now you know I'm encouraging you to do so – you'll need a framework that synthesises what we've been discussing into a coherent whole. We move now to developing a leadership framework built on the culture of the organisation which will then flow through to the structures: the core values and beliefs, and how they are to be acted out. And in keeping with one of the themes of this book, it will be simple, but far from simplistic.

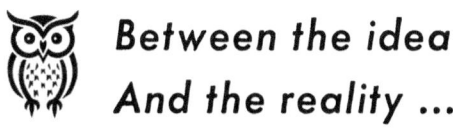

Between the idea And the reality ...

- *Do you experience a tension between urgency and importance in your leadership work? Consult Covey's time management quadrant and do an audit of the time you and your leadership team spend in each quadrant. How often are you in the "important but not urgent" quadrant?*

- *How important do you think the concepts of parallel, distributed and distributive leadership are? Are they already there informally in your decision-making processes? Are there ways you could more deliberately build them into enhancing the quality of your decision-making?*

- *How important do you think the distinction between zero sum and abundance mentalities is in conceptualising leadership, and how power works in your school? Are you prepared to take a deep breath and embrace the abundance mentality? The ingredients are there in your school, waiting for you to bring them together into something unique and special.*

CHAPTER 13
A leadership framework

"You don't have to be Mother Teresa ..."

Your north star

During some of those big-picture sessions, the River Valley leadership team were attracted to Michael Fullan's work on school leadership: in particular his assertion that a school leadership team needs a conceptual framework within which its members work. Without that, Fullan contends, their decision-making will be ad hoc, and some of their decisions may well be unintentionally contradictory to previous decisions, resulting in a lack of coherence and meaning for the school community.

Fullan suggests that the conceptual framework needs to reflect the beliefs and values of the members of the leadership team, and more widely, of the school community; otherwise it will just be words without substance, and will eventually break down or be ignored (Fullan, 2001, 2020). In essence, Fullan is asking leaders and their communities to answer the question we identified earlier – *Why are we here?* – and to ensure that their leadership framework is grounded in their own and the school community's answer.

That takes us back a step. As a school leader, first you'll have to answer that question for yourself. As Harvard educational psychologist Robert Kegan puts it:

> Wherever you go, there you are.

Or as Roland Barth, founder of the Harvard Principals' Centre, words it:

> You can't check yourself out at the schoolhouse gate.

And an existential challenge from the former CEO of Xerox, Ann Mulcahy:

> Who you are, what your values are, what you stand for ... They are your anchor, your north star. You won't find them in a book. You'll find them in your soul.

Just for good measure, in case you're thinking this is a recent idea about leadership, Shakespeare knew it over three centuries ago:

> This above all: To thine own self be true.

We'll develop this further, but for now just remember that this is not "warm fuzzy stuff": acknowledging where we've come from helps clarify where we might be heading, and reminds us there is timeless wisdom to be found in the past if we look for it.

A leadership framework

The River Valley leadership team had explored a number of frameworks, thought about devising their own, and ultimately decided that the one Michael Fullan proposed in *Leading in a Culture of Change* (2001) is an authentic reflection of how they conceptualise their work, and of their personal and team beliefs and values about leadership. The framework as presented by Fullan in 2001 appears here:

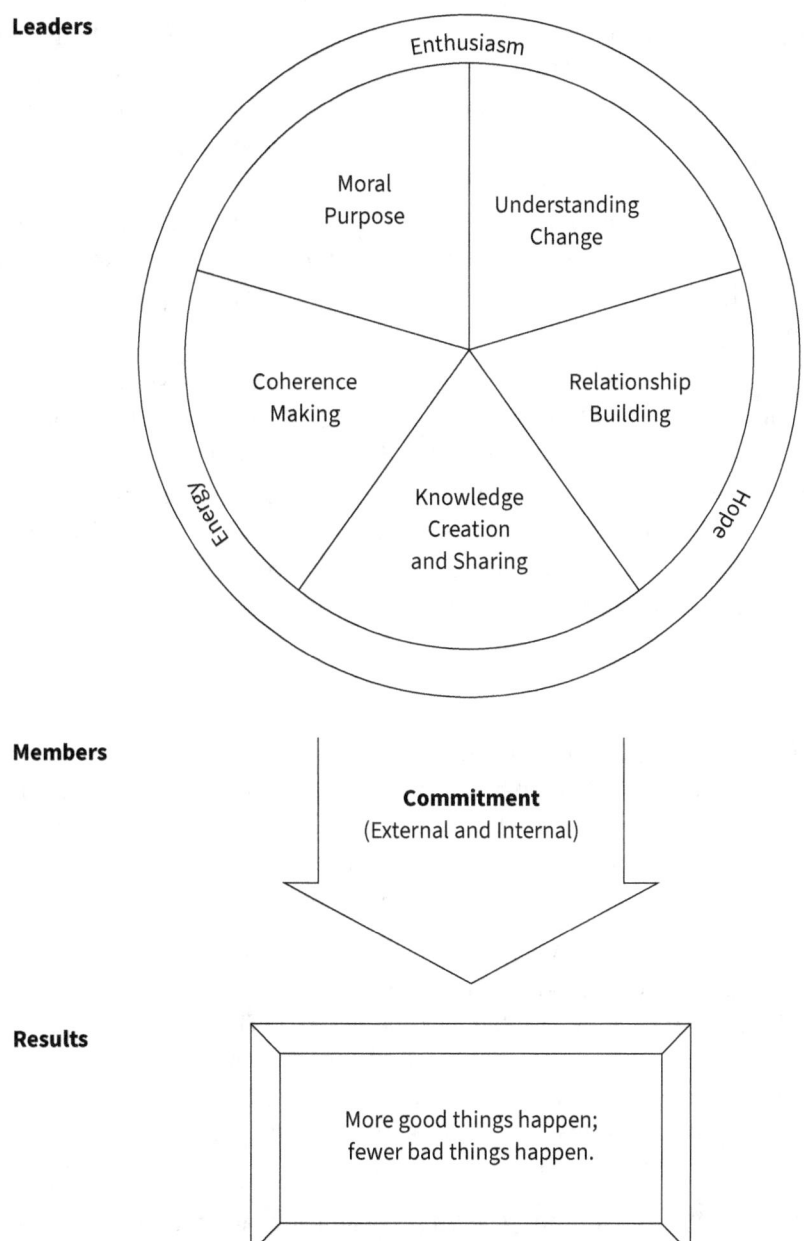

A leadership framework

Twenty years later, Fullan published a second edition of the book, which was reaffirmed by the River Valley leadership team. The 2020 leadership framework remains very similar to what it was in 2001, with the word "nuance" added to "Understanding Change", "Relationship Building" becomes "Relationships, Relationships, Relationships", and "Knowledge Creation and Sharing" changes to "Deep Learning". "Moral Purpose" and "Coherence Making" remain unchanged. In essence, after 20 years of further research and thinking, Fullan and his team found that relationships are even more important to leadership than they thought they were in 2001, change is more complex, and "Deep Learning" better captures the idea of knowledge creation.

One thing about this framework that impressed the leadership team was the wording of the final intended result, as shown in the visual of the model. If the model works to its maximum effect, *More good things happen; fewer bad things happen*. That, to the leadership team, is an acknowledgement of reality, written by someone who understands schools and education systems. Even when you've put in your best effort, you have to expect that some things are still going to go awry. The wildness is always lying in wait.

Moral purpose

Fullan asserts that the effectiveness of the framework depends on accepting that everything in it emanates from the component at 11 o'clock on the diagram: *moral purpose*. That brings us close to what the River Valley leadership team are experiencing in deliberating about Emily's marijuana leaf. It is clearly about more than structures, rules, policies or strategic plans.

> You don't have to be Mother Teresa to have moral purpose. Some people are deeply passionate about improving life (sometimes to a fault, if they lack one or more of the other four components of leadership …). Others have a more cognitive approach, displaying less emotion but still being intensely committed to betterment. Whatever one's style, every leader, to be effective, must have and work on improving his or her moral purpose. (Fullan, 2020, p. 19)

Taking a different tack but travelling the same journey, Simon Sinek has also researched and designed a framework for successful leadership. Referring to leadership and decision-making as "the infinite game", Sinek, like Fullan, offers a framework consisting of five interrelated components, and like

Fullan, he suggests that within the five there is one that is the key driver: he calls it a "Just Cause".

> A Just Cause is a specific vision of a future state that does not yet exist; a future state so appealing that people are willing to make sacrifices in order to help advance toward that vision ... Though we may not like the sacrifices we make, it is because of the Just Cause that we feel it's worth it. (Sinek, 2019, pp. 32-33)

Though the language changes, there is a fundamental symmetry across the two frameworks: both use a circle as their visual, implying the metaphor of a journey that doesn't end, looping back to where the journey begins. Further, each has five elements. The major symmetry across the two models, though, is their conclusion that what underpins the framework – the key driver – is an ethical or moral imperative. When it kicks in to the living, breathing life of the school, this is the fundamental principle for those who lead its decision-making.

I've researched other leadership frameworks, such as that of Mike Edmonds (2018), and those that relate easily to a school situation always come back to moral purpose, though the language might vary. But that's not the end of the story. As we've noted, we can simplify a complex issue, but it's never simplistic. What happens when the moral purpose is clear, but finds itself enmeshed in the age of ambiguity? J. Robert Oppenheimer found himself facing that dilemma when he led the Manhattan Project in the 1940s, developing the weapon that would end the Second World War with the greatest devastation ever unleashed on a country in the history of the world. Oppenheimer clearly saw the ambivalence among his colleagues about the implications for humankind of the devastating power they were looking to unleash. In his own words:

> A subject is much harder to understand when no-one understands it. (Oppenheimer in Gardner, 1995, p. 102)

Oppenheimer had to address for himself the answer to *Why are we here?* Howard Gardner describes how Oppenheimer addressed ethical issues about the bomb's potential when they were presented to him by colleagues on the project. He was a renowned listener, and acknowledged the dilemma. At the same time, he put to those colleagues that if the Nazis developed the atom bomb first, the result would be unthinkable for the future of the world. And he knew the Germans had the intellectual wherewithal, because only a few years earlier he'd been working with their top physicists, sharing their discoveries. Oppenheimer seems to have taken both a short-term and long-term moral purpose in reconciling the *Why are we here?* question. For the Manhattan Project, the answer was to devise the bomb before the Nazis, in order to save the world from the horror of Nazism. The world after the war was a separate issue, to be addressed when the Nazis were defeated.

The Nobel Prize-winning physicist I. I. Rabi, who worked on the Manhattan Project, said of Oppenheimer:

> [He] created an atmosphere of excitement, enthusiasm, and high intellectual and moral purpose that still remains with those who participated as one of the great experiences of their lives. (Rabi in Gardner, 1995, p. 96)

Note Rabi's reference to intellectual and moral purpose in the one sentence. While he was overtly decisive on the moral purpose of the issue, in private, shared with only those closest to him, Oppenheimer felt deep ambivalence about what might happen after the war, when other countries had the same technology. He knew how difficult global co-operation would be because it involved trust among the leaders of nations that had deeply divided ideological views on how a society should be conceptualised and governed. It was now beyond an intellectual issue of science: it was about moral purpose, involving the future of humankind on this planet.

Oppenheimer seems to have understood the interconnectedness of things, and was able to bring people with him, successfully navigating the challenges of decision-making in an age of ambiguity, albeit at great personal cost to himself. On reflection, you'll see that in addressing the competing issues pervading the Manhattan Project, Oppenheimer was engaging in the management of meaning. He was putting the case that while on the one hand this weapon had the potential to destroy the world, on the other hand that was more likely if the Nazis developed it first. It was a nuanced intellectual and ethical argument, far from a binary right-or-wrong decision. As Rabi explained above, there was an intellectual purpose and a moral purpose, and they were layered in ambivalence and nuance. Whether Oppenheimer made the right call is still debated among ethicists today, but a call had to be made, and he made it. And as he pointed out, his role was to lead the development of the bomb: he had no part in the decision of whether or not to use it. (Oppenheimer met personally with President Truman to express caution on its use.)

As school and system leaders it's good to know that we won't have to make decisions that have the moral burden Oppenheimer carried in leading the Manhattan Project. At the same time, it's important to acknowledge that our decisions will at times be laden with the kind of competing moral perspectives that he had to work through. It's a fact of life in an age of ambiguity. He simplified those perspectives through the management of meaning, but it was never simple, and the personal toll was significant. Just be prepared at times for the kind of ambivalence Oppenheimer faced – the nuance amid complexity – and be prepared to accept a personal cost. Above all, take the time to understand the issue's complexities and contradictions. They're always there, and you'll find them if you accept that they're there and look for them before taking a final decision.

You can choose the frameworks of Fullan, Sinek or Edmonds, or those of other writers and researchers, but you can't escape the reality that if you want to be a successful school leader and decision-maker, you must have for yourself, your leadership team, and your school community, a meaningful and coherent answer to the question, *Why are we here?* and be able to articulate it with clear thinking, as Oppenheimer did. Whether you're leading in a religious-based or secular school or system, from your answer to that question, invoked by your values and beliefs, flows your moral purpose, led by you, expressed in a leadership framework with words that capture the spirit and context of your school or system. That is your investment in the quality of leadership you're offering, and indeed in your own sense of fulfilment, achievement and purpose in your work. That is your management of meaning.

> *... if you want to be a successful school leader and decision-maker, you must have for yourself, your leadership team, and your school community, a meaningful and coherent answer to the question,* Why are we here? *and be able to articulate it with clear thinking.*

*

Having come this far, are you feeling a sense of guilt, pressing you to put this book aside now and go back to your to-do list and get on with the busy work that needs to be done in running a school? Is it calling on you to "Just do it", perhaps demanding "a little less conversation"? If so, please pause. Look at it this way: You are not "running a school"; you are leading a community, and leading it in the age of ambiguity. As a school leader, you have significant responsibility for the human development and wellbeing of the young people and the adults in that community. If you listen, you'll hear it calling you to think deeply about what you're doing and why you're doing it, engaging your tortoise mind, not just your hare brain. If necessary, go back a few chapters and check in with Abraham Lincoln and Albert Einstein, or J. Robert Oppenheimer in this chapter: they really did know a few things about decision-making. Or walk a little on Country with Miriam-Rose Ungunmerr-Baumann and see if something of the spirit of *dadirri* finds its way into your thinking.

It took the River Valley principal and leadership team some years before coming to the realisation that they needed a conceptual leadership framework, articulated and drawn from their shared values, beliefs and experiences, guiding the way they believe these need to be acted out in the life of the school, with moral purpose as the driving principle.

I'm inviting you to consider whether you and your leadership team have come to that realisation yet. If you haven't, please give it serious consideration. A lot of research and my own mindscapes and experience suggest that it will guide you in your thinking and decision-making in ways that will help you to convey consistent, coherent meaning and purpose for your school community. The thing is, your leadership framework is already there collectively in your and your community's heads, running around in your hare brains and quietly maturing in your tortoise minds. It's also there in the expectations people have about your leadership, probably tacitly, and while their ways of seeing it may be different from yours, I'm confident that the common ground will be there if you look for it. Peter Block expresses something of that here:

> Leadership is about intention, convening, valuing relatedness, and presenting choices. It is not a personality characteristic or a matter of style, and therefore it requires nothing more than what all of us already have. (Block, 2008, p. 85)

By taking the time to clarify your thoughts and finding the words to capture "what all of us already have", finding the words that articulate your leadership framework and formally and informally sharing it, you'll create a shared conceptual framework. That is a very powerful way to lead and to make decisions.

*

We'll pick up on this theme a little later. We're going to move now into Eliot's shadow, de Hooch's half-hidden rooms, and what happens in the minds of the Peruvian villagers: the places where culture dwells, and where you have to go if you're to make wise decisions for your school community.

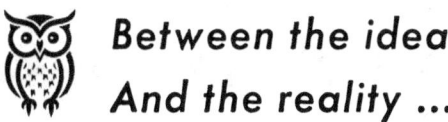

Between the idea
And the reality ...

- *What do you think about the idea of moral purpose as the prime driver of a leadership framework? Can you identify if it's there in your current thinking about your leadership?*

- *What do you make of J. Robert Oppenheimer's decision to take both a short-term and long-term moral position on "Why are we here"? Was he separating the pragmatic from the theoretical, or was there perhaps more to it than that?*

- *Peter Block challenges widely held beliefs about leadership, stating "it takes nothing more than what all of us already have". What do you think about that?*

- *Try to find time to watch the 2023 film* Oppenheimer, *and discuss it with colleagues. Historians affirm its essential accuracy, and it captures much of the complexity and nuance that characterise decision-making in today's world.*

CHAPTER 14

Culture (1):
The art of the covenant

Wisdom and meaning from 1992

Think back to the River Valley team's decision to "sleep on it". We're returning now to *dadirri*, and Guy Claxton's metaphor of the hare brain and tortoise mind. This is where that decision by the River Valley leadership team to set up big-picture thinking and reflection days begins to pay off. Seemingly paradoxical, those once-a-term sessions were deliberately not action-oriented: they were focused on big-picture thinking, aimed at enriching their leadership capacity by accumulating a store of understanding, meaning and wisdom in preparation for the complexity they knew they would have to address sooner if not later. Let's track some elements of that journey.

In agreeing that their decision-making processes were going to be grounded in moral purpose, they set about exploring what this meant for River Valley High. And that sent them into thinking beyond what was immediately visible: in de Hooch's half-revealed rooms, in Eliot's "shadow", and especially in the minds of the Peruvian villagers. What they found there led them to culture, and how important it is to decision-making in the school community they were serving.

*

What does this thing we're calling "culture" actually look like? Often we sense it before we can see it or understand it, and it takes time and some coaxing before it will reveal itself fully. It's the *beliefs* – those things we have decided are true; the *values* – those things we have decided are important and good; and the *norms* – "the way we do things around here", acting out – or not acting out – those values and beliefs (Deal & Peterson, 2016).

The River Valley leadership team is venturing bravely into ambivalence, uncertainty and mystery, but they do so with quiet confidence, because they have a framework they believe in, and an understanding and acceptance about the context they are working in – an understanding and acceptance that has been made easier since three members of the leadership team separately attended the Harvard International Summer Institute for School Leaders some years back. For each of them there were required readings in preparation for the course. One of these, *Moral Leadership* by Thomas Sergiovanni (1992), resonated particularly strongly with the team. Despite the revolutions, evolutions and other changes that have taken place since the book's publication, the team feel that Sergiovanni was offering wisdom and meaning that is timeless, and it resonates with them today.

A "covenant"

Sergiovanni writes that schools in which students flourish academically, personally and socially usually have something in common: what he calls a *covenant*: an agreed set of values and beliefs that are timeless, that engage the heart and the hand as well as the head, and will prevail amid change and complexity. And the covenant is consistently acted out through a process of *purposing*: "the continuous flow of conscious decisions that are consistently coherent and reflecting the covenant" (Vaill, 1984, p. 57).

You'll recall that one of the segments in Michael Fullan's leadership framework is *coherence making*. Fullan combines the spirit of Sergiovanni's covenant and Vaill's purposing when he writes about "shared depth":

> Coherence is not alignment. The latter consists of the rational organisation and explanation as to what the main pieces of the organisation are and how they relate to each other: vision, goals, strategies, finances, accountability, training, and so on ...
>
> Shared depth is not something you can get from a document, a rousing speech, or even a good professional learning experience. I only know one way to shared, collective understanding, and that is through purposeful, day-to-day interaction. Coherence making is a cultural phenomenon. It is what you experience on a daily basis in the setting in which you work. (Fullan, 2020, pp. 119–20)

Three statements from three respected researchers and writers about educational leadership, one writing 30 years after the other two, all saying the same thing – perhaps we should take notice.

*

Look back to the words of William Stafford in "The Way It Is" in Chapter 6. He refers to a "thread", and "While you hold it you cannot get lost". Surely Stafford's "thread" resonates with Sergiovanni's *covenant*, and Fullan's *shared depth*, generating the organisation's sense of coherence: a moral purpose sitting firmly in the centre of the school culture; a widely understood, consistent, clearly articulated and acted-out set of values, beliefs and norms, all modelled by the organisation's leadership team day by day, even in the smallest of interactions.

So I'm saying the "soft stuff" – the culture – is actually the "hard stuff" – the culture drives the structures and they work together. We'll explore this further in the next chapter, working toward a deeper understanding of the kind of thinking that will reward you with sound decisions that are widely supported, and with fewer things going wrong.

> ... the "soft stuff" – the culture – is actually the "hard stuff" –
> the culture drives the structures and they work together.

The long and winding road we're travelling continues to evolve, and in the next few chapters we're stretching out further on the elusive concept of school culture. As I've intimated, you'll find it if you're prepared to look for it, and then you'll find the words to articulate it. A word of caution: whether you choose to look for it or not, it's there. And for better or worse, right now it's impacting on every decision you make.

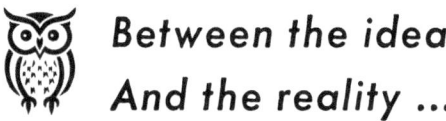
Between the idea
And the reality ...

- *Does your school have a "covenant"? Whether formally or informally, it almost certainly does, and it's sitting in your mind, in the minds of your leadership team colleagues, and in the minds of the staff and wider community of your school or system. The "thread" is in there. Can you identify it amid the clutter of the daily "busy work" that constantly calls for your attention, and can you find the words that capture it?*

- *You should dig deep for those words and find them, because they will guide your decision-making towards working in the higher levels of leadership. It's all there in the hearts and minds of you and the school community, waiting for you to uncork it. And when you do, you'll have engaged in a sophisticated exercise in the management of meaning. That's leadership.*

CHAPTER 15

Culture (2): Walking in two worlds

> "Culture in successful organisations arises in the yeasty crucible of meaning, somewhere between mystery and metrics. It is the glue, the hope, and the faith that holds people together."
> – Terrence Deal and Kent Peterson

Having read the previous chapter, you'll see immediately that we're in complex and nuanced territory when we start to unravel a school's culture. How do we interpret and make meaning out of that "yeasty crucible of meaning" which lies "somewhere between mystery and metrics"? Where is it; and how do we even look for it?

Purposing again

As I've already hinted, it's right there waiting to be discovered, just as Alexandra Horowitz found in that walk with her dog. In schools it's especially there in the little things – the purposing – like the ways the principal and other leaders interact with teachers, support staff, students and parents, and the way teachers relate to one another and to students and parents. It's there in the way students interact with one another: older to younger and vice versa; boys to girls and vice versa; how students with disabilities or gender identities different from the mainstream are treated by the principal and school leadership, the staff, and other students. It's there in the weekly newsletter, and when the principal, leadership team members, and teachers and student leaders address school assemblies. It's there in the stories, some true some apocryphal, told by school leaders, staff, students, parents and alumni. It's there in the timetable, and in those things that receive a lot of attention or reward, and those that don't. It's there in the priorities reflected in the budgeting process and in the budget itself. And it's there in the way mistakes are handled by the school leadership, whether made by students or adults.

Paradoxically, while all those things are there, right in front of our eyes, that doesn't necessarily mean we can see them. It's like looking at one of Pieter de Hooch's half-revealed rooms. How can we see into all the hidden spaces of a loosely-coupled organisation? And it's like the shadow in Eliot's poem, hiding the obstacles that lie between the idea and the reality. That's partly because the culture isn't one singular entity. It's many elements in the life of a school – some small, some large – most of which we can observe singly, many of which we would hardly give a second glance at; and some of which lurk tacitly in people's heads, like the Peruvian villagers' belief about hot and cold. It's when we put them all together in the spirit of Senge's systems thinking that we can look around the corner and see into the hidden room, bring light into the shadow, and start to make meaning from them. And when we can make meaning from them, we can engage in the management of meaning for the school community; for that way lies our ability to lead and make decisions in the age of ambiguity.

"Data driven" or …

In that Peruvian village, the solution to their problem was there, available to them. Part of it was scientific, and some of it was unscientific. Somehow the way forward lay in taking both into account, but no one found a way to do that, because they didn't look for it. Let's move now to something that might appear to make sense on the surface, but also holds secrets in its shadow or its half-revealed rooms. How often have you been told that your organisation needs to be "data driven"? That the way to improve student learning, achievement and wellbeing lies in gathering and analysing the available data – the "hard data"? Indeed the assumed link between measurement and organisational improvement developed into memes in the 1980s, variations of which are still prevalent today. Like this one:

> If you can't measure it, you can't manage it.

Or another popular version:

> What gets measured gets done.

Or this from a US Department of Education spokesperson in 2007:

> If it can't be measured, we're not interested in it. (in Deal & Peterson, 2016, p. 5)

It's a managerial delusion clinging to the hope that leadership is a technical exercise, excusing leaders from having to deal with the human dimension of the school they lead. But they do have to deal with the human dimension, and if they don't they will fail. The assumption that everything of value and importance about an organisation can be measured as "hard data" is a delusion. Metrics are indeed helpful when used intelligently, but on their own they can be like trying to pierce the darkness in Eliot's shadow by holding a match rather than a powerful torch. We need a framed reminder on our wall: "It's the culture, stupid".

In *The Tyranny of Metrics*, Jerry Muller refers to "metric fixation" as one of the most prevalent mistakes made by organisational leaders today:

> The most characteristic feature of metric fixation is the aspiration to replace judgement based on experience with standardised measurement. For judgement is understood as personal, subjective and self-interested. Metrics, by contrast, are supposed to provide information that is hard and objective. (Muller, 2018, p. 6)

Based on my experience, my reading, my emotions and my intuition, I'm confident to suggest that the best organisations are not data driven; they are values and beliefs driven, and data informed. That means human judgement, informed by metrics, is the key to decision-making. When relevant, and when analysed and interpreted in the unique context of the school or system, data can be very helpful in identifying what's working well and where action or change is needed. But that's where the culture kicks in. The "hard" data are important, but not more important than the values, beliefs and norms that ultimately underpin leadership decisions about how the data are used: these are the "soft" data, and they are too often dismissed by "no nonsense" action-oriented leaders.

> *... the best organisations are not data driven;*
> *they are values and beliefs driven, and data informed.*

In the previous quote, Muller uses the key word that all leaders must understand: a decision is not a scientific or mathematical calculation; it's a *judgement*. School leaders would certainly be foolish to ignore relevant data. That's the "metrics" part of Deal and Peterson's quote at the beginning of this chapter. But just what that action should be and how to go about it introduces the "mystery": the other part of that quote. The seductive call to be data driven is a trap waiting for leaders who are desperately wanting it all to be simple – about the metrics – avoiding the mystery where the real substance is. And that part is complex because it lies hidden in the "yeasty crucible of meaning": the culture. And here's the thing: culture, at its deep core, is not about data, it's about people.

*

Let's take that further. Chris Argyris and Donald Schön have offered wisdom to deepen our understanding of what lies behind "the way we do things around here": how the idea finds its way – or doesn't – through to the reality. They delve into what is at work beneath the systems and structures of an organisation, referring to "organisational knowledge", which, they say, is embedded in routines and practices, and can be "inspected and decoded", even when the people acting on them are sometimes unable to articulate those routines and practices in words (Argyris & Schön, 1996).

Two worlds

Those routines and practices are the norms of the school's culture. But if we are unable to put the "organisational knowledge" in our school into words, how are we to understand it? Argyris and Schön suggest we start by drilling down and stretching out on how the formal and informal systems and structures interact with the culture. To do that, we conjure again the formula of "simple but not simplistic", and return to the work of Sergiovanni, who has written about schools and education systems as having a *lifeworld* and a *systemsworld*, concepts borrowed from the German philosopher Jurgen Habermass. The two "worlds" speak for themselves:

> When we talk about the stuff of culture, the essence of values and beliefs, the expression of needs, purposes and desires of people, and about the sources of deep satisfaction in the form of meaning and significance, we are talking about the **lifeworld** of schools and of parents, teachers and students ...
>
> The **systemsworld**, by contrast, is a world of instrumentalities, of efficient means designed to achieve ends ... The former is a world of purposes, norms, growth, and development, and the latter is a world of efficiency, outcomes and productivity. (Sergiovanni, 2000, p. 5)

Sergiovanni goes on to emphasise that both the lifeworld and the systemsworld are necessary for a school to function effectively, and that the two "worlds" need to be balanced and complementary. But he adds a telling rider for school leaders: the lifeworld should drive the systemsworld, in purpose, strategy, decision-making and day-to-day practice in the school. It doesn't take much to link that with purposing, and with the school having a covenant. The lifeworld of the school is the key, and the systemsworld's role is to complement and support it.

The essence of the dilemma facing the River Valley team in determining how to respond to Emily's assignment cover is that every element of the issue that they have explored dwells in one or the other of Sergiovanni's worlds, and sometimes in both. Furthermore, in some scenarios the two worlds are potentially in competition with each other, so the question facing the team is whether they can find a way to combine both the lifeworld and the systemsworld in their decision-making; or will they have to move exclusively into one of those worlds at the expense of the other? They will need to engage in skilful management of meaning here, for themselves and for the school community.

Argyris teases out this potential tension through the terms *espoused theories* and *theories-in-use* (Argyris, 2000). He maintains that these concepts are crucial to the coherence and consistency that are necessary for leaders to be able to manage meaning amid complexity, ambiguity, and competing aspirations in their decision-making. Essentially, Argyris is referring to the congruence or difference between the stated purpose of the organisation – *the idea* – and what is acted out – *the reality*. He highlights the fact that in their decision-making, what an organisation's leaders say, and what they actually do, are sometimes different, and can at times be contradictory. He goes on to point out that if the espoused theory and the theory-in-use differ from each other or are contradictory, it is the theory-in-use that will dominate how people respond, and from which people will take their meaning. In today's language, it's about "walking the talk".

Sometimes this potential dichotomy manifests itself in a crisis, and the organisation reverts to defensive measures, ignoring its espoused theories and revealing its theories-in-use. Peter Weir's film *Dead Poets' Society* offers a fictional example of such a scenario. The opening scene shows the school principal speaking to students and parents on the first day of term, proudly espousing the school's core "pillars" – its espoused theories – held up by students on banners: *Tradition, Honour, Discipline* and *Excellence*. When a student takes his own life, the school leadership ignores its espoused theories as paraded on the flags – in particular, *Honour* – closes ranks, and contrives to make the boy's English teacher, John Keating, the scapegoat for the tragedy. Its theories-in-use are shown to be the dominant driver, contradicting the espoused theories, and the real culture of the school is revealed for all to see.

At times, a school might deviate from its espoused theories because of what it sees as external pressures that force it to compromise those theories. Some such pressures are evident today. Externally imposed examinations continue to be the dominant model of summative assessment in Australia for Year 12 students, despite the known limitations; this form of assessment restricts the ability of students to show what they have learnt, and the ability of teachers to deploy their "unique pedagogical gifts" to meet their students' differing needs (Crowther & Boyne, 2016). The external pressures are also there when standardised test data are used by politicians and the media to make invalid judgements about the quality of schools and systems, and when media-constructed league tables draw superficial and unfair conclusions about schools and systems from the data, or use OECD test data to draw spurious conclusions about whole countries' education systems.

Those perceptions are the result of the data-driven mentality, yet schools are not factories, they are places of human development: of potential, not product. And most of the learning comes from the lifeworld. Think back to what you have brought with you from your school experiences. Are they predominantly about the results of tests and examinations? Or are they mainly drawn from the human life of the school, the relationships between teachers and students, the way the school leaders made decisions, especially when students got it wrong; about fairness, respect, trust and honesty? About the role-modelling of the adults and older students? About how students who struggled academically and students who excelled were treated? Did your deepest learnings come from the school's systemsworld or from its lifeworld?

Gathering and interpreting data serves a positive purpose if the data are used for the purpose for which they were intended to be used. That's a universal principle, and for schools it's to identify areas where school and system leaders and their teachers can work more effectively with their students and with one another. If the school leadership decides to react to the invalid use of data by applying it to teaching and learning, the metrics become the dominant element in the school's culture, including how it presents itself to the community. When that happens, in Sergiovanni's words the systemsworld has "colonised" the lifeworld, diverting the school's direction from its compass – its core values and beliefs – to the detriment of the students and adults in the school. Deal and Peterson describe the process of "colonisation" elegantly:

> Many schools have drifted from traditional cultural roots. In many instances they have lost, or are in danger of losing, their souls ... What were once joyful places of promise and hope have too often become semi-mechanised factories bent on producing only a small fraction of what a well-educated person needs, and, deep down, what a community or the country really wants or needs. (Deal & Peterson, 2016, p. 5)

We leave the "data driven" or "data informed" discussion for now. If you still believe that "If you can't measure it you can't manage it" is your leadership mantra, just be aware that while your focus is on the systemsworld, the lifeworld of your school is happily – or unhappily – moving on without you. Be careful: the wildness is lying in wait for you.

*

> Every word has consequences. (Sartre, 1945)

Argyris and Schön have noted the importance of words in decision-making and communication, challenging the language widely used today in organisations. That particularly applies to schools, especially in the ways we describe student learning and achievement. In some cases I believe the consistent use of particular words today is contributing to the "colonisation" of the lifeworld by the systemsworld, and that's echoed by many school leaders and teachers in Australia. We're still not listening to Argyris and Schön, who told us 30 years ago, "To treat an organisational entity as an impersonal agent is to adopt a kind of machine language ..." (1996, p. 5).

Does that resonate with you? Here's one reason why it should: as Jean-Paul Sartre, quoted above, knew: words are important because they generate metaphors in people's minds. Yet hardly anyone – among education bureaucrats, policy makers, the media, even educators themselves – seems to pause and question using a word like "outcomes" to describe students' learning and achievement. It's as though learning has some kind of finished product; as though it's coming out of a machine in a factory. Every teacher knows there are no outcomes in education: education is a continuing journey of learning. That's the metaphor. It's developmental and complex, never complete. It's transformational rather than transactional. It was expressed well over 30 years ago by Harvard educational psychologist

Robert Kegan: "The more we learn, the more we learn that there's more to learn" (Kegan, 1994). That's why the fad of "outcomes-based education" was such a predictable failure and has taken its rightful place in the dustbin of failed education fads. It's time for the word to join it there.

A further example of machine or factory language in education is the continuing reference to "delivering" curriculum. A curriculum document can be delivered, but that is different from the living, breathing, complex, organic, reciprocal process that teachers and students engage in every day based on that document. That process is *curriculum*, and no-one can "deliver" it. We can offer it, and teachers often have to dig deep into their professional expertise and use ingenious strategies to engage their students; yet we hear "deliver" used regularly, unquestioningly and mindlessly in reference to curriculum. Again, it's the transactional language of the factory, not the transformational language of learning, and it trivialises the complex art and science of teaching in the eyes of the general public. And as with "outcomes", it's regularly used today by educators themselves.

Is it too much to ask that as educators we use the language of learning and leave the language of production to industry, which is its rightful place? If educators themselves use that language, we can't object when bureaucrats, journalists, politicians and others use it. We are the ones who have shown the way.

> *Is it too much to ask that as educators we use the language of learning and leave the language of production to industry, which is its rightful place?*

This is important because, as Sartre pointed out, the words we choose have consequences. They affect decision-making in our schools, bureaucracies and education systems, and in the minds of the general public. The wrong words generate the wrong metaphors in people's minds, influencing their mindscapes and mental models, which capture the way we see the world. And it's insidious. Indeed, we've seen that as far back as 1996 Argyris and Schön were warning us that the misuse of language in organisations – not just schools – has already moved from the factory floor to the technology on people's desks:

> With the pervasiveness of computers in organisations comes a tendency to employ computer language to refer to phenomena that used to be

attributed to thought, will, deliberation, feelings or habits … The power of the computer metaphor may underlie the growing tendency to treat organisations and their parts as impersonal agents. (Argyris & Schön, 1996, p. 5)

That was offered to us back in 1996, and we now have artificial intelligence software that can write papers and reports so convincingly contextual that it's almost impossible to discern whether a human being contributed any actual research or thinking to them. And what an AI program produces is significantly linked with the words we feed into it. Words do indeed have consequences.

It's surely time to consider whether the systemsworld is in the process of colonising the lifeworld of our schools, ably assisted by the words we educators use ourselves. It's likely we're hampering educational leaders and teachers in making decisions that develop and enrich a school culture with a moral purpose that is alive and responsive, and that draws in the students and adults as they engage communally in learning together. That's transformational. The transactional language of the factory won't do it. Are our words helping prepare young people for the challenging world of the age of ambiguity, or for a soulless, data-driven society? A machine can do the latter … if we let it.

*

We're about to move now to one of the fundamental elements of a healthy society, a healthy school culture, and indeed, a healthy relationship.

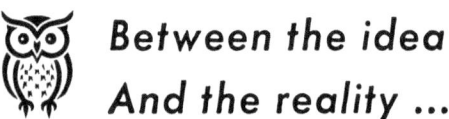

Between the idea
And the reality …

- *Words generate metaphors – word pictures – in people's minds, so the way we use words is fundamental to the management of meaning. Leaders work to build a sense of coherence and clear purpose in the lives of their communities, and the words we use are an integral element in this, directly influencing the decisions we make, how we communicate them, and how they are received. Maybe an audit of the words that roll off your tongue at school assemblies and in staff meetings, and in your written communications like the weekly newsletter or memos to staff, would reveal something about the culture of the school. Do your words lean more to the lifeworld or the systemsworld? Is it mostly the language that describes an alive, organic community, or is it more soulless bureaucratic language devoid of any human identity? It's important, because ultimately your words reveal your moral purpose, and that sets the standard for your school community.*

CHAPTER 16

Culture (3): The power of trust

> "Trust matters. Trust comes from being part of a culture or organisation with a common set of values and beliefs. Trust is maintained when the values and beliefs are actively managed."
> – Simon Sinek

Though he only served one term, Abraham Lincoln is widely viewed as America's greatest president. In September 1862, during the racially-charged years of the American Civil War, Lincoln made a pledge to introduce an Emancipation Proclamation to end slavery, and to do so in three months' time on New Year's Day, 1863. Doris Kearns Goodwin writes that there was widespread cynicism among the public about the likelihood of Lincoln actually keeping his word:

> Critics predicted that its enactment would foment race wars in the South, cause Union officers to resign their commands, and prompt 100,000 men to lay down their arms. The prospect of emancipation threatened to fracture the brittle coalition that held Republicans and Union Democrats together. "Will Lincoln's backbone carry him through?" wondered a sceptical George Templeton Strong. "Nobody knows". (Goodwin, 2018, p. 230)

One person believed he did know. The prominent abolitionist Frederick Douglass had been strongly critical of Lincoln, accusing him of deliberately delaying the issuing of the Proclamation. In late 1862 Douglass was asked by a journalist if he thought Lincoln would renege on his pledge to introduce it just three months away on New Year's Day, 1863. Douglass's response:

> Abraham Lincoln will take no step backward. If he has taught us to confide in nothing else, he has taught us to confide in his word. (Goodwin, 2018, pp. 230–31)

That statement came from one of Lincoln's harshest critics, an African-American who had escaped slavery in Maryland only a few years before.

What would politicians give today to have such an expression of trust come from one of their most vocal opponents? The level of trust in Lincoln, from political allies, opponents, and the general public, is widely reported in research (e.g., Alvy & Robbins, 2010; Burns, 1990; Goodwin, 2005, 2018; Keneally, 2003). And was Douglass's trust in Lincoln's word justified? Lincoln signed off on the Emancipation Proclamation on New Year's Day, 1863, as he said he would, and as Douglass believed he would.

"That one thing is …"

We revisit the River Valley leadership team now as they continue to deliberate on how to deal with Emily's assignment cover. Based on the advice they have received from staff, they know that whatever their decision, not everyone will agree with it. How, then, do they ensure that their decision will be supported by the school community? Perhaps the best way to achieve that would be to take a lesson from Abraham Lincoln 150 years ago, and more recently by Stephen Covey Jr:

> There is one thing that is common to every individual, relationship, team, family, organisation, nation, economy and civilisation throughout the world – one thing which, if removed, will destroy the most powerful government, the most successful business, the most thriving economy, the most influential leadership, the greatest friendship, the strongest character, the deepest love … That one thing is trust. (Covey, 2018)

I've learnt that those words are true, and they go some way to answering the question. If the River Valley principal and leadership team have been able to build networks of reciprocal trust across the school community, then it's likely their decision will be respected. Even if some disagree, as they surely will, most will trust that the decision was taken with integrity, and to the best of the team's ability.

*

I had an early inkling of the power of trust in leadership and decision-making during my time in the armed forces, though I was too young at the time to fully understand how important that experience would be. In 1967 and '68, during the Vietnam War years, I was conscripted into National Service and spent two years in the Australian Army. After six months' training, it was my good fortune to be posted not to Vietnam but to the

Education Section of the 1st Pacific Islands Regiment (1 PIR) in Papua New Guinea: an almost all-native infantry battalion based at Taurama Barracks near Port Moresby. Australia was sponsoring Papua New Guinea to nationhood through the United Nations Organisation Trusteeship Council, and that included responsibility for training the armed forces. Part of that training was an education program, taught almost exclusively by young teachers like me, conscripted into National Service.

In those two years I became familiar with the culture of the Australian Army, finding more subtleties and nuances than appear on the surface. While it is essentially a top-down command system with structures to support that, I found that the culture differed significantly from one battalion to another, depending on the leadership approach of key people. In the two different postings I experienced – Singleton in New South Wales and Port Moresby in Papua New Guinea – this was strongly apparent. Singleton had an authoritarian, unquestioning, at times brutal culture, faithfully implemented by many – though not all – people of rank, driven largely by external motivation based on positional authority. As a member of the battalion rugby team, which comprised mostly regular soldiers and some officers, I picked up that the battalion was not a happy place, and morale was quite low.

Six months later, in the Pacific Islands Regiment, despite the same systems and structures, the culture was vibrant and uplifting, with widespread trust bestowed on people by their superiors, including on young, inexperienced teachers. Like Singleton, it became clear to me that this culture was driven by people in key positions in the regiment, and that this was why morale was high in 1 PIR. (One of the company commanders, Major Michael Jeffery, went on to be Governor-General of Australia.)

My response to this organisational culture as a 21-year-old teacher was to be highly motivated and committed to my work and be accountable for it. It also aroused the thought in my mind that I could lead. I was elected captain of the battalion rugby team, despite the team containing some high-ranking officers. At training and on the playing field, they deferred to me. Back at the battalion, I deferred to them. All this was unspoken: it just happened naturally. What I didn't understand at the time was that this came from the top, and it was deliberate. It didn't just happen.

That cultural experience is something I've taken with me throughout my life, especially in my years as a high school principal. It was only later that I fully understood how powerfully the culture of the 1 PIR battalion was grounded in the network of trust and respect embedded by those in leadership roles, and how that multiplied and generated internal motivation and commitment throughout the battalion to the deeper purpose of our work. The structure and systems were the same in both battalions: it was the culture that drove the motivation and commitment.

*

We move now to another military experience relating to structure and culture, this one from the United States. In *Turn the Ship Around*, David Marquet offers a compelling example of the power of trust, embedded in parallel and distributive leadership. In the foreword to the book, Stephen Covey describes the day he spent on the *Santa Fe*, the United States nuclear submarine commanded by Marquet:

> Throughout the day, people approached the captain intending to do this or to do that. The captain would sometimes ask a question or two, and then say, "Very well". He reserved only the tip-of-the-iceberg-type decisions for his own confirmation. The great mass of the iceberg – the other 95 percent of the decisions – were being made without any involvement or confirmation by the captain whatsoever ... The crew was amazingly involved and there was constant low-level chatter of sharing information. I can't say I actually saw the captain give an order. (Covey in Marquet, 2015, pp. xix, xx)

"I can't say I actually saw the captain give an order." That is an astonishing observation about the functioning of a military structure that is essentially based on command. Covey, a researcher and writer on organisational behaviour, surmised that this was related to the change in culture brought about by Marquet's leadership style. He asked Marquet what underpinned his leadership framework. Marquet:

> My definition of leadership is this: Communicating to people their worth and potential so clearly that they are inspired to see it in themselves.

That is exactly what I experienced as a young teacher serving in the command structure of the Pacific Islands Regiment: "communicating", "people", "worth", "potential", "inspired": five words contained in one sentence that encapsulate Sergiovanni's lifeworld, using the kind of language to capture the culture the captain wanted for his crew. And Covey didn't see him issue an order all day; all this in the top-down command structures of the

United States Navy. It was a culture built on a network of reciprocal trust across the ship. I experienced such a culture at 1 PIR: a context in which I wasn't expecting to experience it, and it has been a defining influence in my professional life.

Can you see the resonance with what we've been exploring, and in particular with the quote from Stephen Covey Jr earlier in this chapter? Everything about decision-making that happened at 1 PIR and on the *Santa Fe* was based on culture, not structure: the trust of the Colonel and the Captain toward their people, including trust in their potential; trust and respect from the battalion and crew toward the formal leadership, and from soldiers and crew members toward one another. You might ask, "Ok, but that's the soft stuff. How would they perform in a conflict situation?" It's a valid question. While the Pacific Islands Regiment has never been tested in battle, for the *Santa Fe* the answer is unequivocal: within a relatively short time, after several simulated battle scenarios, the *Santa Fe* moved from being rated bottom of the nuclear submarine fleet to rating at the top in most criteria of effectiveness. That is a significant achievement, and the key message we can draw from it about the power of trust in the decision-making processes of an organisation is surely something that every person who aspires to leadership simply can't ignore: it's something everyone who aspires to lead should understand and harness.

The success of the *Santa Fe* is a great story, but we need caution here. Marquet's achievement in turning the culture around in such a short time is exceptional. Changing structures is easy: changing culture isn't, and research indicates that it usually takes several years. Perhaps the short time it took to turn the *Santa Fe* around was partly due to the smallness of a nuclear submarine's crew, and the uncomplicated nature of its purpose. For a larger, more complex organisation like a school, such a quick result would be extremely unlikely.

My colleague Paul Browning, ex-Headmaster of St Paul's School in Brisbane, Australia, has written a book based on his doctoral studies. In summing up his findings, Browning writes:

> The building of trust should be the core business of every leader no matter the context: sport, politics, business, not-for-profit, church or voluntary organisations. Once trust is established, it becomes the norm that sets the standard for how employees (both paid and voluntary) behave towards each other and perform their work. Once it becomes

part of the culture of an organisation, trust works to liberate people to do their best, to give others their best, and to take risks and innovate. (Browning, 2020, p. 15)

> *Once it becomes part of the culture of an organisation,*
> *trust works to liberate people to do their best,*
> *to give others their best, and to take risks and innovate.*

That has been my experience. Like Browning, when I came to understand the depth involved in the power of trust, not just in the culture of an organisation or community but also in my personal and social life, I found those words to be true. I think I always knew intuitively that it was so, but it took time for me to realise just how important it was.

Relational trust

In the late 1980s and into the '90s, a great story played out in the United States. The Chicago public school system was performing poorly and the authorities, out of desperation, devolved decision-making across the system to the school level (Russo, 2004). Over a period of 10 years, some of the schools showed significant improvement in their students' literacy and numeracy, and some didn't. On investigation by Anthony Bryk and Barbara Schneider, those schools that improved were shown to have a common characteristic in their cultures that other less successful schools didn't have: a web of reciprocal trust among the adults and the students.

We need to go into Eliot's shadow and de Hooch's half-hidden rooms and take the time to look more deeply at this. Firstly, what do Bryk and Schneider mean by "trust"? As usual in the age of ambiguity, it's both complex and nuanced. Bryk and Schneider did not say all that is needed for students to improve their academic achievement is the establishment of a culture of trust; but it was the trust factor that appeared to be the discriminator among the schools where students improved.

In defining the characteristic they observed in those schools, Bryk and Schneider named it *relational trust*, and offered the following "criteria for discernment" to describe it: *respect, competence, personal regard* and *integrity*, with a particular rider referring to *centrality of the principal*. I won't insult your intelligence by asking which of Sergiovanni's two "worlds" those four concepts reside in, as you'll have already worked it out.

*

In the evolving decision-making process at River Valley High about Emily's marijuana leaf, Bryk and Schneider's "criteria for discernment" are lurking beneath the surface. They're all in the lifeworld, yet at the same time we know that the systemsworld has to be part of the decision too. A data-driven culture can't provide the substance of those criteria in decision-making, but a data-informed culture will contribute to it.

The River Valley problem-solving group have a structure within the school to address the issue they're addressing. The crucial question, though, is: Does the culture have the necessary qualities to inform and empower the structure, not the other way round? Is the lifeworld strong enough to embed the systemsworld with moral purpose, and do so without seriously disrupting the day-to-day functioning of the school? The levels of relational trust across the school community will surely be playing a significant part in that.

"The centrality of the principal"

Let's move to the rider mentioned earlier that Bryk and Schneider place on their "criteria for discernment" for relational trust: *centrality of the principal*. They offer a neat conceptualisation, evoking Argyris and Schön's espoused theories and theories in use:

> Given the asymmetry of power in ... school communities, the actions that principals take play a key role in developing and sustaining relational trust. Principals establish both respect and personal regard when they acknowledge the vulnerabilities of others, actively listen to their concerns, and eschew arbitrary decisions. If principals couple this with a compelling school vision, and if their behaviour can be understood as advancing this vision, their integrity is affirmed. Then, assuming principals are competent in the management of day-to-day school affairs, an overall ethos of trust is likely to emerge. (Bryk & Schneider, 2002, p. 137)

Principals establish both respect and personal regard when they acknowledge the vulnerabilities of others, actively listen to their concerns, and eschew arbitrary decisions.

In a follow-up work to that of Bryk and Schneider, Julie Kochanek researched further on the centrality of the principal in building a culture of relational trust. She found:

> A principal holds formal power over the teachers' positions and informal authority over ... parents who [may] lack an equal education or job status. In this atmosphere, it is incumbent on the principal to reduce the vulnerabilities of others to initiate the growth of trust in the school. The principal is in the best position to bring participants together by promoting ... positive discernments of respect, personal regard, competence and integrity. (Kochanek, 2005, p. 18)

The symmetry in Bryk and Schneider and Kochanek's findings about the centrality of the principal in building trust is compelling, and it matches my experience: the cultures at Singleton and Taurama and on the *Santa Fe* embodied parallel, distributed and distributive leadership, but in each case that was only made possible by decisions made at the top, based on a culture of relational trust.

*

(An aside on "the centrality of the principal": During my time as a principal I was initially surprised at the way my behaviour or my words impacted on people across the school community. At times I was reminded by staff, students or parents of something I had said or done that was important to them, but I'd simply seen it as a normal part of my role, and sometimes hadn't even remembered it. One thing in particular stands out: If someone had contributed to a discussion in a helpful way at a staff meeting, or a staff member or student had exercised leadership when speaking at the weekly assembly, I always took the time – only a few minutes – at the end of the day to hand-write or email a brief note to say thanks. Usually the person read it on arrival at school next morning. The number of times teachers or students said that simple act "made my day" was both uplifting and a bit frightening: I hadn't realised how "the centrality of the principal" was such an important artefact in the day-to-day culture of the school: even in a school where parallel and distributive leadership were embedded in the culture. Fortunately I discovered it early in my principalship, and made sure I was aware of it in pretty much every decision I made.)

Five elements

The power of trust in an organisation's culture that I've offered so far is essentially based on experience and research, some of it dating a fair way back in time. But there's a sense of a story and continuity in these findings, and we turn now to more recent work by Sahlberg and Walker, who write about the importance of trust as a fundamental principle in Finnish culture, including in the education system. They are essentially validating Bryk and Schneider's findings in Chicago with their experience across the Atlantic in Finland.

Without using that language, Sahlberg and Walker make a direct link between the lifeworld and the systemsworld of Finnish schools. They reference the research of Professor Megan Tschannen-Moran (2014) in identifying five elements that together constitute a powerful example of relational trust that, while referring to Finland, more widely characterises schools where students achieve strongly in their academic work. The words are slightly different, but their meaning is unmistakenly in congruence with Bryk and Schneider's "criteria for discernment": *benevolence*, *reliability*, *competency*, *honesty*, *openness* (Sahlberg & Walker, 2021, pp. 23–24).

Choose the language of Browning, Bryk and Schneider or Sahlberg and Walker, and you will still arrive at the same fundamental principles that place trust in such a powerful place in a school's culture. I'm suggesting that for successful decision-making by a leader of any organisation or community, the message is too powerful to be ignored: relational trust needs to be a fundamental element of school culture, especially in the way decisions are arrived at, communicated and accepted (or not accepted) by the school community. And have you noticed the link with moral purpose that weaves its way through all this? Bryk and Schneider, Kochanek, and Sahlberg and Walker are surely saying to us that when relational trust is at work in a school's culture, all students, including those from disadvantaged backgrounds or with disabilities, are likely to improve in their learning and achievement through the decisions that emanate from that culture. Perhaps that is "the thread" which "while you hold it you cannot get lost"?

Walking the talk … or not

The River Valley leadership team understand that whatever decision they make, there is bound to be disagreement in the school community. The advice they've received and the thoughts shared with them by staff and some parents vary between the lifeworld and the systemsworld, but few seem to acknowledge that both worlds are in play with this issue. Even so, most understand that it's difficult and complex. The leadership team know that they don't have the luxury to base their decision exclusively on one world or the other. They have to confront the age of ambiguity and address both.

They will be hoping that their research on the power of relational trust in the school culture and their resultant work in building networks of relational trust across staff, students and parents will land their decision on a base where the decision will be accepted and their integrity in reaching the decision will be acknowledged by the great majority of the school community. They know that leaders who are trusted are people who "walk the talk": their decisions and actions match their words. As we have seen, Argyris and Schön's version of "walking the talk" is where the espoused theories match the theories-in-use. When they are in tune, trust is likely to be alive and well, with all the benefits to leadership that we have just discussed. When they aren't, it's likely the leadership will soon find itself in trouble.

*

I think two key messages for school leaders emerge from all this. The first applies to all organisations; the second is a bonus that applies specifically to schools:

(i) When a difficult decision has to be made and it's likely to disappoint some people, the levels of relational trust across the organisation's community are important if the decision is to gain widespread acceptance and support.
(ii) When a school's culture is grounded in relational trust, students are not only learning an important message about life; their academic learning and achievement are likely to improve too.

*

We close this chapter by returning to Peter Drucker, who often saw things about organisational behaviour a long time before those who work in those organisations, and before other researchers in the field saw them. In a paper first published in 1999 and republished in 2006, Drucker foresaw in all organisations what Bryk and Schneider found a few years later in the Chicago public schools, and what leaders like David Marquet intuitively understand:

> Organisations are no longer built on force but on trust. The existence of trust between people does not necessarily mean that they like one another. It means that they understand one another. Taking responsibility for relationships is therefore an absolute necessity. It is a duty. (Drucker, 2006, p. 16)

Are there principles and learnings here that go beyond schools and related systems, reaching into all organisations, with particular reference to decision-making? Peter Drucker thinks so, and he knew a lot about organisations and leadership.

*

We move now to an element in school culture that builds on relational trust in decision-making, from staff meetings to the classroom to parent meetings, and includes written communication. It will play a role in the River Valley decision, though for some, perhaps many, it will be subliminal rather than at the front of people's minds. I have come to believe that it's an essential element for every school leader's mindscapes/mental models. Read on.

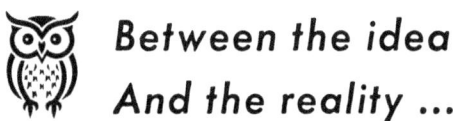

Between the idea And the reality …

- *Stretch out with colleagues on the assertion that "the soft stuff is really the hard stuff". How does this resonate with your leadership experience?*
- *Identify what you see as the various networks in your school or system community. How high would you say the levels of relational trust are within them, and between each one and the others? How well do the networks of trust integrate across the school or system community? How well do the lifeworld and systemsworld work in concert with each other as an organisational whole?*
- *What do you think about Bryk and Schneider and Kochanek's assertion about the "centrality of the principal" in the culture of the school?*

CHAPTER 17

Culture (4):
The power of hope

"If you teach nothing else, teach hope." - Hedley Beare

"Hope is the thing with feathers that perches in the soul,
And sings the tune without the words, and never stops at all."
- Emily Dickenson

When I was a young English teacher in the late 1970s, my Year 10 class was studying *To Kill a Mockingbird*. I felt that some of the historical issues that faced African-Americans at that time had some similarity to those faced by our own Indigenous people. I took a chance and phoned the office of Queensland Senator Neville Bonner to ask if he might spend a lesson with my class to talk about "walking in two worlds". Bonner was the first Aboriginal person to be elected to the Australian Parliament. Despite the demands on a senator in the Australian Parliament, he accepted my invitation.

During the discussion, a student said that he walked early each morning with his father, and under a cross-river bridge that they passed was a group of inebriated Aboriginal men who were always there. He asked Senator Bonner if he knew what might have caused this. The senator paused momentarily, then said, "It's what happens when people lose hope." The sadness and dignity in the way he said those words hung in the air, and the class fell silent for what seemed a long time before one of the boys nodded and said quietly, "I get that." Others nodded; but no-one else spoke until Senator Bonner also nodded and moved the conversation on.

There are some experiences in our lives that we take with us and never forget. That moment is one of mine. It's with me today as though it happened yesterday, and I'm confident it's still there for those students who, I think, realised that they had been part of a special moment in time.

Let's talk about hope, and its place in school leadership and decision-making.

"The certainty that something makes sense …"

We're weaving another thread into the mix that comprises the culture of the school: something every leader needs to hold, and when necessary, fall back on when making decisions that will have school- or system-wide implications and repercussions. It's an example of the nuances that come into play when we choose the words for something that is complex. We're looking at three words in particular that are related but different from one another – *hope*, *optimism* and *belief* – and we're delving into not just the meaning but the spirit of each.

Writing about "the importance of hope in human lives, institutions and society", Frank Crowther and collaborators Karen Fox and Bruce Addison offer a link between trust, hope and decision-making that I suggest is universally true for individuals, schools, education systems, and human relationships in general:

> [Hope] represents the desire for something qualitatively better than the status quo; that it is inseparable from trust; that permeates many of the world's great belief systems; that is basic to everyday planning and goal setting; and, while it can be dimmed, clouded or blotted, it cannot ever be totally extinguished. (Crowther et al., 2021, p. 134)

That is an eloquent statement. I'm going so far as to suggest that leaders who don't work to embed trust, hope, and the close relations of those two, optimism and belief, into their school's culture, are going to struggle to link their decision-making with a moral purpose, thereby greatly limiting the quality and likely impact of their decisions on their school communities. It's part of the "soft stuff" we've been focusing on in these last few chapters.

Let's narrow things down a bit. I've used two words in this chapter that we often assume mean the same thing: *optimism* and *hope*. It might just seem semantic, but I'm suggesting that while leadership needs both, there is a subtle difference, and it's relevant to what we're exploring here. Vaclav

Havel, Czechoslovakia's inspirational leader during the "velvet revolution" against Soviet repression in the 1980s, makes the distinction:

> Hope is definitely not the same thing as optimism. It's not the conviction that something will turn out well, but the certainty that something makes sense regardless of how it turns out. It is this hope, above all, that gives us strength to live and to continually try new things, even in conditions that might seem hopeless. (Havel, 1991, pp. 181-82)

Hope is definitely not the same thing as optimism. It's not the conviction that something will turn out well, but the certainty that something makes sense regardless of how it turns out.

If we genuinely believe that at their most fundamental level schools are places of potential and human development, it surely follows that they will also be places of hope: that deep belief that Havel writes about above: "the certainty that something makes sense". It also begs the question: How do we nurture and strengthen potential and hope when we can't measure or sometimes even see them? In fact, sometimes potential is not always obvious in the young people and adults we work with because, depending on how we decode it, the "hard" data can actually disguise the potential that's hiding in the "soft" data. If we don't show our young people that we believe in their potential and inspire them with hope so they can believe in themselves enough to realise that potential, then why are we doing what we do? Why are we here? What is our moral purpose? We have to trust that it's there, and believe that we can do something about it that will have significance in their lives. That's the espoused theory. Let's pause here to consider our theory-in-use, remind ourselves that we are living in the age of ambiguity, and ask how this relates to the decision-making process regarding Emily's marijuana leaf at River Valley High.

The answer is sitting there beneath the surface, and not far beneath it. The hope, "the something that makes sense", is surely the degree to which the leadership team and their colleagues believe their own espoused theories. In this complex and nuanced situation, how strongly do they actually believe in the "certainty" of Emily's potential as a young human being? They often speak publicly about River Valley High being a place that discovers and nurtures young people's potential, and that mistakes are learning opportunities. Are they prepared to match those statements with their theories-in-use by treating Emily's mistake as an educative issue, not just a punitive one? And if they do, how do they also ensure that the message goes out to the school community and on into the wider community that River Valley High is true to its espoused theories but also strong in its approach to illegal drugs?

It's time for another thinking expedition. We're about to tap into another Ancient Greek myth and research based on it; we then travel to Copenhagen to take in a unique Danish concept; then to Las Vegas to see the legacy of a champion tennis player; and finally to Sydney, Australia, where a refugee has an uplifting tale to tell. And they all go to the heart of decision-making. I did warn you: this is a long and winding road we're travelling.

The Pygmalion effect

In Ancient Greek mythology, Pygmalion was a sculptor. From a piece of ivory, he sculpted a woman who was so beautiful that he fell in love with her. He kissed her lips, and to his wonderment and delight they were warm and welcoming. His expectation that she would respond to his deep expression of love was so strong that his sculpture had come to life.

In the 1960s, Robert Rosenthal and Lenore Jacobsen pursued the possible truth that lay behind that story, and explored the potential power of teacher expectations in student learning. Published in 1968, *The Pygmalion Effect* has had a major impact on educational thinking. Because of its continued success, the authors continued their research and updated the work in 1992.

Rosenthal and Jacobsen were studying the potential power of teacher expectations to create "self-fulfilling prophecies" in students, and had embarked on a research project in a primary school in outer San Francisco. At the beginning of the year, researchers told teachers that based on "a test for academic blooming", certain students in their classes showed the potential to "spurt" and improve significantly in their academic achievement over the coming year. And that is what happened. Then the researchers revealed that there was no "test for academic blooming": those students had been selected at random from the group. Just as Pygmalion conveyed such strong expectations for his sculpture that she came to life, the teachers' belief in the potential of those particular students, based on the "test for academic blooming", appeared to have a similar impact on their achievement.

The claims by the researchers were challenged by other researchers who suggested it was just another example of the well-known Hawthorne Effect, but the integrity of the findings has held up over time. Thus the power of teacher expectations as it relates to young people's potential achievement has entered the pool of knowledge and understanding about pedagogy, and *Pygmalion in the Classroom* has become a classic in educational research.

Can you see this relating to Vaclav Havel's definition of hope? To the teachers, the *something* in "the certainty that something makes sense" was their belief – based on what they thought was authentic data about the potential of those students – that the students could do what they were expected to do. And they did.

Rosenthal and Jacobsen's work focused on the academic achievement of students. But what if we pose a follow-up question: Could the Pygmalion effect go beyond intellectual achievement and also apply to young people's personal and social development, including what happens when they make a mistake? After all, George Bernard Shaw's play *Pygmalion* and Lerner and Loewe's musical *My Fair Lady* are based on that assumption. If it might be true, how important to their decision-making is the way the River Valley leadership team conceptualise and act on Emily's mistake, and others like it? Do their espoused theories really match their theories-in-use?

Dannelse

On study leave in northern Europe some years ago I spent a week in Denmark, visiting schools and meeting with academics, mostly in and around Copenhagen. I was interested in the distinctly different Scandinavian concept of leadership, and wanted to see if it might apply to student leadership in Danish schools. On one occasion early in my visit I sat down with Professor Leif Moos, an academic at the Danish University of Education, and asked him to explain for me the basic philosophy underpinning Danish education. He said it was difficult, because it's based on a Danish concept that has no direct English translation: *dannelse*. Moos explained *dannelse* by describing students as the "not-yet" people: they are still becoming who they will be, and teachers and parents in Denmark hold that as a fundamental belief about their young people. There is no "hard data" to prove it; it's "soft stuff": a cultural belief in "the certainty that something makes sense regardless of how it turns out". It's an example, from the deepest level of a country's culture, of Havel's definition of hope.

Fables again

As synchronicity would have it, the week I was in Copenhagen coincided with the celebration of the 200th birthday of Denmark's most famous and celebrated author, Hans Christian Andersen. Every school had displays in the library and in classrooms depicting his stories and characters, and there were celebrations in the streets with music, drama and dance. At one of the schools, the principal was at pains to explain to me that Andersen actually wrote those stories for adults as well as for children: they are fables meant to have relevance for an adult audience, just like Aesop's stories. She urged me to read Andersen's stories in direct translation from their original text, so I visited a local bookshop the next day and purchased an unedited English translation.

That evening I sat down and began reading the stories. I soon came to "The Ugly Duckling", and on finishing it I had a sense of déjà vu. And the penny dropped. Hans Christian Andersen has written a fable about *dannelse*. The duckling who is ugly and different and rejected by the others turns out to be a beautiful swan. Denmark's most famous writer has captured the essence of the fundamental "something that makes sense" for Denmark's educational philosophy: the deep cultural belief that this is not the finished product here in our classrooms. It's *dannelse*: the "becoming", "not-yet" person. That one word – "yet" – conveys the hope the Danes hold for the potential of their young people. It's more than optimism. This is a nation's deeply held framework driven by a moral purpose, expressing an unfailing belief in the potential of its young people.

Though it might not be an exact parallel, the spirit of *dannelse* has been recognised outside of Denmark, including by two leaders widely respected in their own countries and internationally:

> Education is the great engine of personal development. It is through education that the daughter of a peasant can become a doctor, that the son of a mineworker can become the head of the mine, that a child of farmworkers can become the president of a great nation. It is what we make out of what we have, not what we are given, that separates one person from another. (Nelson Mandela, 1997, p. 194)

Education is the great engine of personal development.

And:

> We were given dedicated teachers, first Mr Martinez, and then Mr Bennett, both gentle and good-humoured African-American men, both keenly focused on what their students had to say. There was a clear sense that the school had invested in us, which I think made us all try harder and feel better about ourselves. (Michele Obama, 2018, p. 45)

Those excerpts speak for themselves, but if you check for the most-used word in the excerpt from Nelson Mandela you'll see that it's "become". And while Michele Obama's words imply it without stating it, there is no mistaking her thinking: she titled her autobiography *Becoming*, and one of her key themes is the way people believed in her potential as she made her way to becoming one of Chicago's most respected lawyers. *Dannelse* is at work beyond Denmark.

I think *dannelse* is a beautiful concept: one for all leaders, not just school leaders and teachers, and should be an integral element in the mindscapes of all leaders. In its own way it's probably already there with you in your mindscapes, and has played a role in guiding you into the teaching profession. As Argyris and Schön remind us, though, when we're making decisions in a context of complexity and nuance, it's not always easy to match the espoused theories and theories-in-use. I'm sure the Danes would want us to start with *dannelse* whenever we make decisions about difficult behaviour or a struggling student. Will it reflect Havel's concept of hope and be the "something that makes sense"? Will the moral purpose prevail over easier structural solutions? And of particular relevance to us, will it permeate the deliberations of the River Valley leadership team and their colleagues as they work through to a decision?

Believe

And now for the third word I mentioned at the start of this chapter: *belief*.

A few years ago, my wife and I travelled to Las Vegas for the wedding of a nephew. I had arranged for us to spend a day at the school that tennis champion Andre Agassi established in suburban Las Vegas: the Andre Agassi Preparatory Academy, a K–12 Charter School only a few kilometres out from "the strip". You don't have to go very far out to find yourself in the real Las Vegas. The school is set in an area that has been traditionally characterised by low income, low education levels, youth crime, and low expectations for its young people. It's here that Agassi grew up. In his autobiography, *Open*, he says that if it wasn't for tennis he almost certainly would have lost his way in his early teenage years, as many of his friends of the time did.

It's evident before you even enter the school. Your eyes immediately go to a large window at the entry, most of which is taken up with one word etched on it. I'll let Agassi tell you himself what it is in a moment. Agassi's tennis achievements include the "golden grand slam" – Wimbledon, the US, Australian and French Opens, and an Olympic gold medal – yet he says these are minor achievements compared to the school he founded in 2001. In his own words, he is "a ninth grade dropout whose proudest accomplishment is his school".

As we walked around the campus and dropped in on classes, a sense of hope and belief in the potential of the students was palpable. Without using those words, the Pygmalion effect and *dannelse* are clearly core values in the culture of the school. On a wall in the entry is a plaque showing how to donate to the foundation that funds the school. Its heading: *With education there is hope.*

As we walked from the elementary school to the middle school, the symbolic messaging was unambiguous. The grounds are designed like a college campus, and little niches and welcoming common areas appear in unexpected places. What Agassi describes below matches what we experienced:

> Everywhere you look are little touches, subtle details that signify this school is different, this place is about excellence, through and through. On the front window is etched one large word, our unofficial school motto: BELIEVE …
>
> The walls are stone – muted purple and pale salmon quartzite from local quarries – and the walkways are lined with delicate plum trees, leading to one beautiful holly oak, a symbolic Tree of Hope, which we planted even before the ground-breaking. First things first, our architects figured, so they planted the Tree of Hope, then asked construction workers to keep the tree watered and lighted while they built the school around it. (Agassi, 2009, p. 380)

In the same courtyard, on a patch of grass not far from the Tree of Hope, is a bronze sculpture of a man dressed in worker's clothing holding a hose, watering an imaginary garden. Las Vegas is in the middle of the Mojave Desert, so the dual symbolism of bringing life – physical and intellectual – into the desert as an expression of hope and belief in the potential of young people is unmistakable. Many of the students are African-American, so Agassi asked the architects to embed bricks of marbled glass into a wall, depicting the Big Dipper, and to the right one single brick of glass, representing the North Star. He explains how the Big Dipper and the North Star were beacons of hope for runaway slaves, pointing them to freedom. If you don't know where you've come from, you don't know where you're going.

Following formal street signage, we walked along Endeavour Boulevard, Discovery Way, College Street, Excellence Lane, and crossed into Achievement Lane to enter a display area that features floor-to-ceiling visual depictions of Martin Luther King, Nelson Mandela, Mother Teresa, Mahatma Gandhi and Amelia Earhart. Below each photo, on raised glass, is an inspirational quotation from the person, each in some way or other expressing hope and belief through language about aiming high, perseverance, care and respect for others, all with an underlying message of belief. Among the photographs is the now famous image of New York firefighters defiantly raising the American flag amid the rubble of the terrorist attack on New York's Twin Towers on 11 September 2001.

The teachers we met were quietly but strongly committed to what they were attempting, and expressed unfailing belief in its importance and in their ability to make it happen. I was left in no doubt that the culture of the school and the decisions made by its leadership marry their espoused theories with their theories-in-use. We met up with students from prep to high school as we moved around the school, and they consistently made eye contact and greeted us in a relaxed, respectful way. Some engaged us in talking about Australia, exhibiting curiosity, quiet confidence and enthusiasm about the school. Our lasting impression was that the power of hope and belief in the potential of young people is firmly and genuinely at work here, and having a powerful impact on the students' lives.

I share the experience of that day in Las Vegas with you because the Andre Agassi College Preparatory Academy seems to be getting so much right, especially in the thinking that went on before the big, and even the little, decisions were made. In *Open* Agassi goes into some detail about this, and it's clear that knowingly or unknowingly he and his fellow planners followed Abraham Lincoln's sharpening of the axe before using it, and Albert Einstein's 55:5 minutes formula for making decisions. The school is a living, breathing testament to deep thinking, optimism, hope, and trust in what can be achieved if the belief is clear and strong enough.

Agassi doesn't directly refer to moral purpose, but identifying and harnessing the potential of young people in a disadvantaged area before their circumstances can cause them to be lost or enticed into negative pathways is surely a clear example of the concept. And I was left in little doubt that it is embedded in the school culture as a "covenant", reinforced through "purposing", as defined by Sergiovanni and Vaill in Chapter 14.

There is something special, deep and abiding in the fact that one of the greatest tennis players of all time, living in a home full of trophies to prove it, sees his greatest achievement as a school offering hope for young people from disadvantaged backgrounds, based on belief in their potential. I wonder if it leaves you feeling inspired too.

"The Secret Drama Teacher"

From Las Vegas to Sydney. In an interview with Robert Macklin, the celebrated Australian raconteur, artist and comedian Anh Do, a refugee to Australia after the Vietnam War, relates a seminal incident that would ultimately shape his future:

> In Year 8, the school did a weird thing. It decided that half the class got to do drama and the other half had no potential. The drama teacher walked in and began to select his "chosen class".
>
> He called out a bunch of other boys' names, but there was still a slim chance, three spots left ...
>
> Not me ... damn!
>
> Not me ... damn!
>
> Not me, again. Bloody Hell. My heart sank. (Anh Do in Macklin, 2006, p. 96)

As is the case in so many instances of a school streaming or tracking students on their so-called "ability", a structural approach usually based on "hard data", Anh Do accepted the school's judgement that he had no talent in drama. Then fate intervened:

> One day Mrs Borny, our English teacher, walked in and decided us bunch of rejects weren't hopeless and started to run her own drama classes. She never agreed with splitting the class up in the first place,

and even though she'd never taught drama before, she improvised and pretty soon we were doing our own version of plays and acting games. Suddenly this bunch of rejects felt like the lucky ones, the ones taught by "The Secret Drama Teacher" ...

One day she said to me, "Anh, you're a very talented story teller". She had no idea how far that one line of encouragement would take me. (Anh Do in Macklin, 2006, p. 97)

Until Anh Do met Mrs Borny years later through another turn of fate, as is the case with so many teachers and students, she didn't know the impact her belief in his potential had had on his life, and the school's decision-makers would never have known of the loss to the world their decision-making had almost caused (unless they had read Robert Macklin's book). Just like Eliot's shadow and de Hooch's half-hidden rooms, to the decision-makers the impact of those decisions was invisible on the surface.

How much educational and leadership theory was acted out in those two examples of decision-making – the first impacting temporarily in a negative way, the second permanently in a positive way, on one young person's life? Listen to Mrs Borny's response when Anh Do, now famous, caught up with her many years later on an episode of the Australian television series "Thank You":

> I walked up to her, gave her an enormous hug and told her about everything she'd done for me. She held me tight around my waist and said to me, "Anh, Anh, I'm so proud of you. So proud of you".
>
> She was surprised and shocked and couldn't believe that I'd even remembered her. I told her that it was her who convinced me I could write, that it was her who told me I was a good story teller. I also told her that I was but one of probably thousands of kids whom she'd impacted with her kindness and that she was my Robin Williams character from "Dead Poets Society". Tears welled up in her eyes. (Anh Do in Macklin, 2006, p. 98)

Have you heard a more inspirational story of hope and belief by a teacher? The thing is, seemingly minor interactions like that happen every day in the life of a school. That's the "soft" power of belief and hope, and you won't have missed that the Pygmalion effect was alive and well in that story. Everything changed in one young man's life because of a decision based on the mindscape of one teacher. What if that teacher's mindscape was embedded in the culture of every school, and decisions by the formal leadership were based on it?

Fixed or growth?

Most educators are familiar with Carol Dweck's work on mindsets. We're in the territory of mindscapes or mental models and their impact on decision-making. Dweck's research and thinking have led her to conclude that people hold one of two mindsets about their own and others' capabilities: *fixed* or *growth* (Dweck, 2006). Essentially, Dweck's message lies in the power of hope and belief, and it was Anh Do's good fortune that Mrs Borny understood this, because the school's leadership didn't.

Much of Dweck's work focuses on young people and their teachers or parents, with stories of students who failed because they – and their teachers – believed their abilities were "fixed", and others who succeeded because they – and their teachers – believed they had the ability to grow their intellects and their innate talents. And those most responsible for those young people who had the "growth" mindset are their teachers, parents and caregivers. Especially their teachers, as exemplified through Mrs Borny. And perhaps there's a hidden corollary here: that teachers need to have that belief about themselves, not just about their students:

> Mindsets frame the running account that's taking place in people's heads. They guide the whole interpretation process. The fixed mindset creates an internal monologue that is focused on judging: "This means I'm a loser". "This means I'm a better person than they are …"
>
> People with a growth mindset are also constantly monitoring what's going on, but their internal monologue is not about judging themselves or others in this way. Certainly they're sensitive to positive and negative information, but they're attuned to its implications for learning and constructive action. What can I learn from this? How can I improve? (Dweck, 2006, p. 215)

Dweck's focus is on how a growth mindset influences intellectual development and academic achievement of students, but some of her language suggests broader relevance. As we did with the work of Rosenthal and Jacobsen, what if we take Dweck's thesis to include young people's personal and social development? And those of the adults in the school? If it works with intellectual intelligence, could it also work with emotional and social intelligence? And that leads us to Daniel Goleman.

Goleman's Emotional Intelligence Competence Framework for the workplace comprises five "competencies": *self-awareness*, *self-regulation* and *motivation* – about the self – and *empathy* and *social skills* – about relationships with others (Goleman, 2006). Goleman's book is about relationships with others, yet three of the five competencies he suggests leaders and managers need are about the self, and only two relate to others.

So we return to what I hope is now a familiar theme. If an educational leader's mindscapes conceptualise schools through a growth mindset of hope and belief – as essentially places of potential – where does this leave our leadership team at River Valley High in dealing with Emily? And where does it leave you in your day-to-day decision-making, in your personal and social relationships, including your workplace? Which mindset are you coming from?

To conclude this chapter, I'm handing the final words to Andre Agassi, whose school is surely an unambiguous example of Dweck's growth mindset, and a powerful expression of Vaclav Havel's definition of hope:

> The place is still freshly painted and pristine, just as sparkling as it was on opening day. Students, parents, the neighbourhood, everyone respects the school because everyone owns it. The area hasn't completely rebounded since we arrived. While I was giving a tour recently, someone was shot across the street. And yet in eight years not one window has been broken, not one wall has been sprayed with graffiti. (Agassi, 2009, p. 380)

In the next chapter we explore something that acts on everyone's mind, every day. It's always present, waiting for its opportunity to kick in. It's especially active when we're making a decision. It's complex and tricky, and it's there with the River Valley leadership team as they move towards a solution to their dilemma.

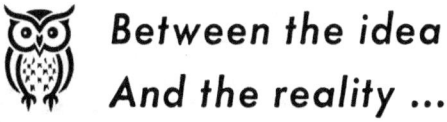

Between the idea
And the reality ...

- *Brainstorm with your colleagues on ways that your leadership practice can articulate and act out the idea of hope as "the certainty that something makes sense" in the culture of your school or system community. Can you identify the "somethings" and build them into the culture, including in your decision-making?*

- *Are there ideas from the way the Agassi school uses symbols and artefacts that you can use in your own school?*

- *The school Ahn Do attended in Sydney made a policy decision – streaming/tracking of students based on the (fixed mindset) assumption that standardised test performances are the main indicator of a student's innate ability. That decision had a significant impact on one student's perception of his capabilities (as decades of research have suggested it would). Then a teacher made a (growth mindset) decision that had an even greater impact, pointing the direction for the next stage of his life. Have a conversation with colleagues about how those two mindsets might be present in the culture of your school or system: include assumptions made about the adults as well as about the students.*

CHAPTER 18
Intuition (1)

"Far from being monochrome, the palette of human understanding contains a variety of ways of knowing – ranging from pure acts of intuition through to exercises in judgement and in the scientific method – which must be combined if we are to make sense of the world." – Henry Ergas

We come now to perhaps the most puzzling and difficult element in decision-making; something we may not always be aware of, but which is in action every time we make a judgement. We're talking about intuition. It's the "gut feeling" we all experience in personal and professional situations, particularly when complexity or emotions are involved. That makes it integral to pretty much every context in our lives, especially our decision-making.

It's elusive, complex and tricky: elusive because it's hard to pin down; complex because researchers in the area acknowledge that we still don't fully understand how it works; and tricky because it can work in unpredictable ways on our thinking. There isn't even agreement on what it is, or where it comes from. It's multi-faceted, with some facets sometimes in competition with others; and often we don't even realise it's there, stealthily finding its way into almost every thought process we're experiencing. That's why it's impossible to ignore, because whether we like it or not, intuition is always there in the "wildness lying in wait". Stretch out on it with me now. We'll draw from research, literature, philosophy, and my own personal experience as we delve into the mysterious "something" we call intuition.

> *... whether we like it or not, intuition is always there in the "wildness lying in wait".*

In previous chapters I've made occasional references to intuition, usually accompanied by a note of caution. That caution is about relying too much on intuition when making decisions, because in one sense it's an abstraction, but at the same time it's important to recognise and acknowledge its presence and its impact on our thinking.

We're going to analyse it by exploring three questions: *What is it? Where does it come from?* and *What are we to do with it?* But first, let me tell you about my Don Quixote experience. It's a cautionary tale about intuition, and has resonance with the story of Anh Do and his English teacher, but without the happy ending.

Intuition and expectations

This is a story about intuition and mindsets, coloured now by research and hindsight. It was a lesson hard learnt, because it involved the seductive nature of that "gut feeling" we all experience, which has such a deep influence on our thinking. Whenever there is a decision to be made or a problem to be solved, our hare brain quickly latches onto our intuition and begins running around throwing up all kinds of solutions. But at the same time our ever-alert tortoise mind also takes it on board and begins, slowly, to ponder it. I think this is what happened for me as a young English teacher in the early 1970s, when I didn't give that tortoise mind an opportunity to do its work on an issue that was more complex and nuanced than my intuition or my hare brain – or those of my colleagues – were telling me.

In the 1950s, '60s and into the '70s, educators widely assumed that separating students into high-stream and low-stream classes or tracks – those students achieving well and those struggling – would benefit the learning of both groups. I was a typical young high school teacher holding those assumptions, which were essentially based on intuition, not evidence. There was little research into streaming/tracking at the time, and much of the thinking was intuitive or ideological, and fixed rather than growth-based. *Pygmalion in the Classroom* was published in 1968, but was barely known about at the time. If I'd looked further, though, I'd have found that some researchers were beginning to caution that streaming was not so simple, and like the rats of Hanoi, a well-meaning initiative might actually be having unintended negative consequences.

I was only a few years into my career as a high school teacher, and one of my classes was a high-stream English class of 15-year-olds. It was a dream experience, characterised by high motivation, curiosity and very few behaviour issues. Then the next year I had a low-stream English class of the same age group, and it was close to a nightmare. Low self-esteem, low self-expectations, and poor behaviour were the norm, with minimal achievement in their academic work: not just in my classes, but also in those low-stream English classes taught by my colleagues. How could that be, when our intuition was telling us this will help these kids? Why don't they get it? Surely it's common sense?

Turns out it wasn't. It was intuition, and in this case our intuition was wrong. At the stage those students were at in their development, adolescence has well and truly kicked in, and young people are searching for their identity, the person they are becoming: something clearly understood in the Danish school system through *dannelse*. School is a crucial player in these young people's development because their school is their main community. Values, beliefs, and norms based on them are at work there every day, as they are in every organisation, and students tune in to them, as my colleagues and I soon found out.

No matter how hard we tried to explain that this was good for them and they could do this work, the students assigned to those low-stream classes took one single and very powerful message from the school that outweighed anything we said: "We're dumb. We're losers, not capable of achieving much, so why should we try?" Sadly, that is the unintended fundamental message we gave to those kids, and they believed us. As we saw in the previous chapter, this was Anh Do's experience too until a teacher challenged that assumption and broke through with a more powerful and positive message.

This was many years before Anh Do's experience and many years before Carol Dweck's work on mindsets, but I remember taking on that challenge with a particularly difficult group of Year 9 English students, insisting they could do it and that I believed in them, introducing every strategy I could come up with to engage and motivate them. One was to introduce film, and we watched *High Noon*. The students were captivated as the clock moved toward midday, the time the county marshal would have to face the "bad guys" in the street for a shoot-out. And there was an ethical issue woven into the story. Would the students pick it up? When I set them an essay topic similar to what we would ask of a literary study, their writing was alive, notwithstanding spelling and grammatical errors, though most of the students, when they put their minds to it, showed reasonable competence there.

They also picked the irony and the ethical dilemma in the story: how the marshal's young wife, a Quaker and a pacifist, told him she would leave him if he went into a gunfight in the street, even though he was doing his duty as county marshal to protect the town from having the outlaws take over. When the crunch came and she saw her husband standing alone and outnumbered in the street and an outlaw hiding behind him taking aim to kill him, she picked up a rifle and shot the outlaw. I felt a great sense of fulfilment in the class discussions that followed, and then in what those students produced in the assessment piece. I hadn't anticipated what would come next.

Tilting at windmills

Along with the other Year 9 English teachers, I submitted my gradings to the head of department. A few days later he called me in and told me my gradings were inflated. He showed me a graph of the year group results for that unit of work – other teachers had used different stimulus sources but the questions were the same for all students – and according to my gradings my class had placed above what the other low-stream classes had achieved. The department head told me to go back to the scripts and re-evaluate them, which I did. And I concluded that with an exception or two I'd been pretty accurate against the assessment criteria. I then asked a colleague if he would grade the students' work, and he graciously took the significant time involved to do so. He came back and said he was confident I'd got the gradings pretty much right.

Armed with this affirmation, I returned to the head of department to put the case that my gradings should stand. Like Don Quixote's windmills, he was immovable. Based on their results at the end of the previous year, it was not possible for those students to have achieved those results, and I was to adjust them and move them down. I told him I was not prepared to do so, and handed them over to him to do what he wanted. (That was the first time he'd actually seen any of their work.) A short time later, the year group results were published among the Year 9 English teachers, and my class was level with the other low-stream classes.

Climbing onto the saddle on Rocinante, I brought the issue to a subject meeting where all English teachers were present. Not wanting to lay blame, I put the case that the problem was the streaming of the students and the expectations that flowed from this, because it was based on a predetermined fixed mindset about students' abilities that wasn't necessarily true. I suggested that we should discontinue the policy of streaming English classes and look to research for better ways to meet differing student needs. It was discussed over several subject meetings, then we took a vote. There was majority support for my proposal, though a number of teachers were not supportive of it, with one suggesting I was "rabble-rousing". Most of those teachers who voted against argued for what they saw as the perceived advantages for students in the high-stream classes; they pretty much saw the low-stream kids as "riff raff" and collateral damage: a lost cause because they misbehaved and appeared uninterested in learning.

The subject head was surprised at the vote and found himself in a political situation he hadn't expected and didn't want to be in. He was against the change and took his problem to the principal, who called me in a few days later and respectfully told me the vote was not a convincing enough majority, he was supporting the subject head, and the streaming of English classes would continue. It seemed I was tilting at windmills.

Research prevails over intuition

Unbeknown to me, the school's director of studies, a widely respected educator who was up-to-date with educational research, announced at the beginning of the next year that streaming would no longer be used in allocating students to classes in Years 8 to 10. He referenced research in explaining that with the exception of some mathematics classes, streaming would no longer be an organising device for allocating students to classes. I immediately realised that I should have involved him in the issue during the previous year, but hadn't thought to. (It would appear that the principal took no part in the decision announced by the director of studies, and he may not have even been aware of it. His leadership duties lay elsewhere, and he'd just diverged from those with a quick fix for his subject head's problem and moved on.)

The first English teachers' meeting for the new year began without mention of the previous year's events, and one of the "anti-streamers" from the previous year mentioned that the school had just moved to what the majority of English teachers had been advocating for much of the previous year. There was some mumbling and shrugging of shoulders, and that was it. We moved on, and it wasn't mentioned again. Sadly, though, my previous warm relationships with the subject head and some colleagues were damaged permanently.

Looking back, I think where our intuition initially failed us was in the assumption that if we put all the students who were struggling into one class-sized group we could give them more individual attention. Those assumptions were wrong, and as with the rats of Hanoi, the reality was that the opposite turned out to be the case. All of those students were struggling in different ways, and needed different strategies to help them. Before streaming, they were spread across all the classes, so the numbers in each class were relatively small. With streaming, they were all in one or two classes and the task was too much for one teacher. On top of that, we had unintentionally branded them as "losers", which they unquestioningly accepted.

Before going further, I need to make clear that I think some form of temporary performance grouping of students, especially in mathematics, where building blocks are necessary before further learning can take place, is appropriate. I have seen how students who were slower than others to pick up on basic mathematical principles, when given the extra time and support to consolidate their understanding, have then gone on to rejoin their general classes and successfully handle higher mathematical learnings. The growth mindset is alive and well in those situations. It's the fixed mindset – often based on intuition – that is problematic, with the permanent labelling of young people based on their perceived "ability" at a particular time.

"Ability groups" are not ability groups: they are performance groups, indicative of where a student is achieving at a particular place in time: a long-term indicator neither of a young person's ability nor their potential. If the school leadership make the wrong assumptions, unintentionally telling a young person or a group of young people they are not capable of high-level learning, they will believe it and then find other ways to seek their identity, like misbehaving, or worse still, giving up. As you see, it's directly related to decisions made by the school's leadership, and its effects can be profound.

> *"Ability groups" are not ability groups: they are performance groups, indicative of where a student is achieving at a particular place in time: a long-term indicator neither of a young person's ability nor their potential.*

Forty years after *Pygmalion in the Classroom* was published, New Zealand researcher John Hattie's synthesis of international educational research makes clear that students allocated to low streams/tracks experience significantly negative results in both achievement and equity, the latter sometimes even more strongly than the former (Hattie, 2009). School and system leaders, please take note: intuition in decision-making only gets you so far. You need to do the research, and of course, the thinking.

The power of questions

So let's do some thinking. With the benefit of much experience, research and hindsight, and conversations with teachers over many years including recently, I think I understand what was happening in the experience I've just related. Internationally respected organisational thinker and consultant Peter Block maintains that leaders move too quickly to solutions and leave out the step that should come first: questions. Block asserts that "questions are more transformative than answers and are the essential tools of engagement" before any action takes place (Block, 2008, p. 103). In that spirit, please reflect on these questions about my Don Quixote experience – and not just with your hare brain. I'm confident there will be a good deal of symmetry across your answers.

(i) Can you see mindscapes/mental models and mindsets at work?
(ii) Can you see the systemsworld and lifeworld at work?
(iii) Can you see *Pygmalion in the Classroom* at work?
(iv) How might this story have played out if *dannelse* had been the prevailing assumption about young people?

I understand more about meaning and wisdom after that experience, and I share it with you here because maybe there's some meaning and wisdom in it for you too.

*

It's time to return to the title of this book and home in on the words of T. S. Eliot:

> Between the idea
> And the reality ...
> Falls the shadow.

It shouldn't surprise us that when we bring light into the shadow of an issue, systems thinking comes into play, as it always will. There are connections and nuances that aren't easily revealed, and won't reveal themselves unless we take the time to look for them. The *idea* of giving a student or group of students who are struggling some extra attention holds true – as long as our mindscape is based on the hope and belief that the student can learn, rather than on a fixed mindset about the student's innate ability to learn. Even though our intuition leads us toward the structure of streaming/tracking as the solution, and even though as educators we appear to be applying what we might call "expert intuition", we are well and truly in the darkness of the shadow between the idea and the reality.

So why was our intuition wrong, and why do some leaders today continue to get it wrong in the face of now compelling evidence? In a broad sense, I think our intuition has got it right: based on our values and beliefs, we believe we must do something to help students who struggle. That's the idea. It's the reality that is the problem: this is not about structure, and our mistake was that while our intuition led us to act to help students who were struggling, it also led us to a simplistic structural solution when the way to address the issue was through the more complex and nuanced territory of the school's culture: our values and beliefs and our assumptions based on them.

*

"Complex" and "nuanced": there are those words again. If we're decision-makers in our school, we just can't escape them. Alluding to Sergiovanni's mindscapes and Senge's mental models, Hans Rosling, professor of international health and co-founder of Médecins Sans Frontières, offers further light on why intuitively we can get things wrong even when we have all the information we need to get it right. Using the well-known optical illusion next, Rosling suggests it comes from the way our brains work.

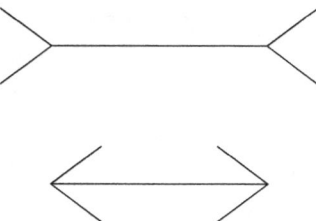

When we look at these two lines, we see the lower line as shorter than the other. But it isn't. They are the same length and we can use a ruler to measure both lines to prove it: that's the hard data. But that doesn't alter the way we see them: when we view those lines armed with the knowledge that they are both the same length, the lower line is still shorter, even when we know it isn't. Rosling explains:

> The human brain is the product of millions of years of evolution, and we are hard-wired with instincts that helped our ancestors to survive in small groups of hunters and gatherers. Our brains often jump to swift conclusions without much thinking, which used to help us avoid immediate dangers ... we have many instincts that used to be useful thousands of years ago, but we live in a very different world now. (Rosling, 2018, p. 15)

Rosling calls these instincts our "overdramatic worldview". He concludes that "our appetite for the dramatic goes way too far, prevents us from seeing the world as it is, and leads us terribly astray" (2018, p. 15). So every time we engage in decision-making, our instinctive "overdramatic worldview" is trying to get into the action. Rosling is surely warning us that sometimes our "gut feeling" can distort our thinking and lead us into poor decisions if we're not aware of where it's coming from and don't have strategies to rein it in and keep it under control.

*

I'm sure you can see where this is heading: we're on the same section of the road where we encountered Aesop's fable, Claxton's hare brain and tortoise mind, Miriam's *dadirri* and Kahneman's "silence in our mind". Jumping straight to a structural solution based on an immediate intuitive thought without an intellectual and emotional balance and taking deliberate time for reflection will sometimes prove justified, but mostly it won't. And those times are where "the wildness lies in wait" and "leads us terribly astray". The quick jump to a structural solution ignores the research-based understanding that the best decisions come first through the culture, then the structures follow. And culture doesn't reveal its intricacies and ambiguities until we take the time to seek them out.

> *Jumping straight to a structural solution based on an immediate intuitive thought without an intellectual and emotional balance and taking deliberate time for reflection will sometimes prove justified, but mostly it won't.*

This chapter has been about a mindscape that includes the Agassi Academy concept of *belief* with Vaclav Havel's conceptualising of *hope* and the kind of *trust* that Abraham Lincoln was able to garner in his decision-making, along with Carol Dweck's *mindsets*. It's a complicated brew, but it helps to deepen our understanding of the intricacies that contribute to our intuition when we're making judgements. And that's especially important to understand when we're making judgements that flow through to decisions.

*

We've noted that Pete Seeger asked back in 1960, "When will they ever learn?" Perhaps the answer is, "When they understand how our minds work, abandon the quick fix, and take the time for complexity and nuance to form meaning in their minds". That doesn't fit easily into a three-minute song, but that's the point: it's not meant to.

Are you wondering what my Don Quixote story and its underlying learnings have to do with the dilemma facing the River Valley High team? Let me assure you that it's highly relevant. It's about the power of expectations, and how that mingles with the concepts of hope, belief and trust, finds its way into the two mindsets identified by Carol Dweck, understands the strengths and limitations of intuition, confronts and rises above the "overdramatic worldview", and ultimately flows into our decision-making. Anh Do was indeed fortunate that his English teacher, Mrs Borny, intuitively understood this when the school leadership didn't.

*

In the next chapter we pursue Pete Seeger's question further as it relates to intuition and decision-making, starting with some questions of our own.

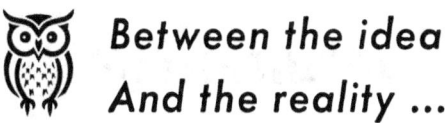
**Between the idea
And the reality ...**

- *Check in with John Hattie's synthesis of educational research,* Visible Learning, *and look up what international research says about the impact of so-called "ability grouping" (streaming/tracking) of students who are judged by their school to have limited and fixed potential in their learning.*

- *What do you think about my suggestion that the power of expectations – the Pygmalion effect – might apply to people's behaviour as well as their intellectual potential? Does it enter into decision-making in your organisation?*

- *Have you ever taken on the role of Don Quixote and found yourself tilting at windmills? With hindsight, what could you have done differently?*

- *What do you make of Hans Rosling's explanation for why people persist with something even when the evidence tells them they've got it wrong?*

CHAPTER 19

Intuition (2)

Following on from Pete Seeger's question, we begin this chapter by asking a "transforming" question:

Intuition: What is it?

> **intuition**: direct perception of truths, facts, etc independent of any reasoning process. (*Macquarie Dictionary*, 2001)
>
> **intuition**: the power of attaining direct knowledge without evident rational thought or the drawing of conclusions from evidence available. (*Penguin English Dictionary*, 2002)

There are some key words here, but let's focus on one for now: *perception*.

> **perception**: an immediate or intuitive recognition, as of a moral or aesthetic quality. (*Macquarie Dictionary*, 2001)
>
> **perception**: an awareness of one's surroundings that is produced by the operation of the senses. (*Penguin English Dictionary*, 2002)

As we've come to expect in the age of ambiguity, there is complexity and nuance in these words. Do those definitions suggest something to you? *Immediate recognition*, which is *independent of any reasoning process*, and making judgements *without drawing of conclusions from evidence available, without evident thought* ... It all sounds very much like Claxton's "hare brain", running fast, full of confidence, ready for action. As we've already seen, though, with intuition the tortoise mind is also in action, slowly and quietly, usually unnoticed unless we're aware that it's there. The same applies for Rosling's "overdramatic worldview", and as we'll see, that's not all. The definitions of those two words – intuition and perception – suggest that there's a lot happening here.

Where does it come from?

Daniel Kahneman is one of the most respected researchers on this topic. Like Henry Ergas at the beginning of the previous chapter, Kahneman suggests that intuition is multi-faceted. To Kahneman, one of the facets is "expert intuition". As an example of this, he documents a true event where a team of firefighters were called to a house where the kitchen was on fire. The firefighters had extinguished the kitchen fire when suddenly one of them shouted without knowing why, "Let's get out of here!" Within a minute the floor collapsed. The source of the fire was not in the kitchen, but in the basement. The firefighter had experienced a "sixth sense of danger". He knew something was wrong but didn't know why (Kahneman, 2011).

That intuitive flashlight seems to have come from many hours of experience in fighting fires. Kahneman suggests the firefighter had become an intuitive expert in his field, and references Henry Simon, a colleague who studies chess masters. According to Simon, something from the firefighter's past experiences, stored in his memory, triggered a cue, signalling danger. Based on that and other instances, Simon asserts that "intuition is nothing more and nothing less than recognition" (Simon in Kahneman, 2011, p. 11).

Kahneman accepts Simon's understanding of "expert intuition", seeing it as something like Malcolm Gladwell's "magic of 10,000 hours" (Gladwell, 2009), which accumulate and culminate in the insights of an expert. However, in a later work, Kahneman (2021) issues a caution about using expert intuition on its own in decision-making. He suggests that expert intuition is one facet of something bigger, more nuanced and complex, with that "gut feeling" going beyond our accumulated past experiences and emanating from other sources, including our emotions. And that leads us to Daniel Goleman and emotional intelligence.

"The sweet spot for smart decisions ..."

Goleman has made emotional intelligence the core of his research and thinking. In *Focus* (2014) he relates a story about Steve Tuttleman, a financial advisor for a major investment group. Tuttleman says of decision-making about major investments: "I bought what *I* liked. I go by my gut". Goleman explains Tuttleman's background, which goes back to a childhood interest in finance, showing that over the years Tuttleman has become an expert in the field, developing "expert intuition"; but Goleman then adds a further dimension, supporting Kahneman's claim that emotion often plays a key role in decisions based on intuition. Referring to Tuttleman's trust in that gut feeling:

> When we make a decision like that, subcortical systems operate outside conscious awareness, gathering the decision rules that guide us and store our life wisdom – and deliver their opinion as a felt sense. That subtle stirring – This feels right – sets our direction even before we can put that decision into words ... gut feelings are data, too ...
>
> The sweet spot for smart decisions ... comes from not just being a domain expert, but also from having high self-awareness. If you know yourself as well as your business, then you can be shrewder in interpreting the facts (while, hopefully, safeguarding against the inner distortions that can blur your lens). (Goleman, 2014, pp. 222–23)

I see Goleman placing intuition within Sergiovanni's mindscapes and Senge's mental models here: the importance of self-awareness: knowing and understanding our personal ways of seeing the world, based on our experiences, our values, and our beliefs. Goleman suggests that being a "domain expert" on its own isn't always the kind of intuition we can trust in making decisions; but it is more likely to be so when combined with high self-awareness. In that case, if Steve Tuttleman consistently makes successful judgements about where to invest large amounts of money, we can assume that his decisions draw from both being a domain expert and having high self-awareness, manifesting as an intuitive "gut feeling". Furthermore, do the phenomena that Goleman refers to above as being "outside our conscious awareness" take your mind back to Guy Claxton's "slow knowing" and Miriam Ungunmerr-Baumann's *dadirri* – residing somewhere in our subconscious, always processing our experiences, and slowly building "our life wisdom"?

Goleman claims that "gut feelings are data too", and makes clear that he sees intuition as a valid and important contributor to effective decision-making. At the same time, it's important to note that he is talking about a nuanced and more complex understanding of intuition than just some mysterious inspiration, gift or feeling coming from within. He also challenges Henry Simon's claim that intuition is "nothing more and nothing less than recognition". For a school leader, there's wisdom here. Making a decision about a complex issue purely on gut feelings, without having the expert intuition developed over time about that issue or looking at the quantitative evidence, or having high self-awareness, is a questionable practice which could end badly.

Even if that financial adviser is unaware of it, expert intuition is an integral contributor to the gut feelings he puts his faith in when making decisions about investing. And if he is unaware of it, the danger for him is that he may lack the self-awareness that is essential in making intuitive judgements, and assume that he has an inherent universal gift for making wise decisions beyond the area in which he has developed his expert intuition. I think I've encountered leaders with this attitude. Perhaps you have too. That's the territory of hubris, and it has undone many a leader. They may indeed have an intuitive "preference", as described, for example, by Myers and Briggs, but to rely on it in every decision they make would be a folly that they may not recognise until it's too late.

*

Intuition, values and emotions are not far apart: indeed, they may all be part of the one entity. Kahneman and Goleman offer important and helpful insight and wisdom about this for leaders grappling with difficult decisions. Just how much weight do we give to our intuition and how much to "hard" data? How much to our intellect and how much to our emotions? How much to our values and beliefs? How much to quantitative data and how much to qualitative data – which may well include intuition? This is where nuance dwells, challenging us to make sense of it. There are no easy steps or blueprints here, and if anyone is still thinking leadership is about quick, action-oriented decision-making and charisma, tread carefully: the wildness has you in its sights and it's lying in wait for you.

In an age when leaders, including school and system leaders, are being urged to lead "data driven" organisations, what Kahneman and Goleman are saying is surely relevant. Goleman's advice that we should include gut feelings as data will be counter-intuitive to some leaders, but it's a concept that calls on us to pause and contemplate. If we follow Kahneman and Goleman's lead and include feelings deriving from expert intuition along with self-awareness as data, we are now conceptualising intuition as being in the domain of mindscapes. They also take in the leadership frameworks we visited earlier, which are driven by moral purpose, grounded in values and beliefs, and acted out through norms that purposefully and consistently model those values and beliefs. This is a conceptually different understanding of "data", and with the research base that it emanates from, it presents a strong challenge to those who reject intuition and emotion in decision-making and call for a clinical "facts and figures", "hard data" approach. At the same time, feelings and facts can give us conflicting messages that generate ambivalence, so caution to allow our tortoise mind to work that through as data is equally important.

> *Goleman's advice that we should include gut feelings as data will be counter-intuitive to some leaders, but it's a concept that calls on us to pause and contemplate.*

*

I know – it's all pretty complicated, but don't let it immobilise you. The key learning, which I'm sure you've grasped, is that intuition is always at work in decision-making, and it's a useful guide to your judgement. At the same time, there are different kinds of intuition, and none of them is an infallible guide. So intuition can be both a help and a hindrance, depending on the context. An understanding about how complicated it can be, combined with your own self-awareness, is enough to equip you to bring some wisdom and caution into your thought processes when making judgements. And at times remind yourself who won that race!

In the next chapter we continue to explore intuition, and visit a controversial novelist and poet and an organisation theorist, both of whose works are read by millions. Our quest for meaning and wisdom continues.

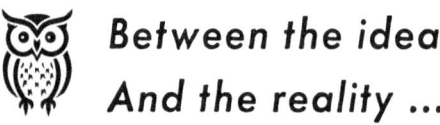

Between the idea
And the reality ...

- *Have you experienced a situation similar to that of the firefighter who called on his team to get out immediately: you sensed that something was wrong (or right), but didn't know why?*

- *Have you ever made a decision about a complex issue based on your gut feeling and found that it was right? Can you articulate why it was right? (You may not be able to.)*

- *Have you ever made a decision about a complex issue based on your gut feeling, only to find that it was wrong? Can you work out why it was wrong? (You should be able to.)*

CHAPTER 20
Intuition (3)

> "What our blood feels and believes and says, is always true."
> – D. H. Lawrence

> "We cannot violate these natural laws with impunity."
> – Stephen R. Covey

We turn now to two authors whose writings have been widely read and discussed. D. H. Lawrence is regarded as one of the 20th century's most important novelists and poets. He is also one of the most controversial. Stephen R. Covey is an organisational researcher and writer who explores organisations and leadership through the mysterious world of metaphysics. Let's explore what they have to say, and think about how it relates to intuition as it applies to decision-making.

"The mystery of the flame"

Consider this, in a letter from D. H. Lawrence, written to his friend Ernest Collins in 1913:

> My great religion is a belief in the blood, the flesh, as being wiser than the intellect. We can go wrong in our minds. But what our blood feels and believes and says, is always true. The intellect is only a bit and a bridle. What do I care about knowledge? All I want is to answer to my blood, direct, without fribbling intervention of mind, or moral, or what-not...

> I conceive a man's body as a kind of flame ... and the intellect is just the light that is shed onto the things around. And I am not so concerned with the things around – which is really mind – but with the mystery of the flame forever flowing, coming God knows how out of practically nowhere, and being itself, whatever there is around it, that lights up. (Lawrence in Hawkins, 1969, p. 371)

Is this about intuition, or do the references to "blood" make it more complicated? If we accept the dictionary definitions at the start of the previous chapter, perhaps Lawrence is writing about intuition. It's passionate stuff, and it goes beyond Simon Henry's claim that intuition is simply memory drawn from experience; it's perhaps closer to Goleman's view on the role of emotion in decision-making. In referring to "the flame forever flowing, coming from God knows how, out of practically nowhere", Lawrence acknowledges that he doesn't really understand this force he's writing about; but at the same time he believes unequivocally in its power and its "truth". That sounds a lot like intuition.

Lawrence's understanding of intuition reads here like a philosophy for living dangerously: to pursue wants over and above needs, with the only moral dimension being in what our "blood" tells us: it's in our DNA. But in another letter, to Mrs S. A. Hopkins in 1912, he writes about his love for his wife, who left her husband and children to go with him:

> Let every man find, keep on trying till he finds, the woman who can take him and whose love he can take ... But the thing must be two-sided. At any rate, and whatever happens, I do love, and I am loved. I have given, and I have taken – and that is eternal. (Lawrence in Hawkins, 1969, p. 371)

Despite his previous passionate words about acting irrespective of moral or other contexts – "All I want is to answer to my blood" – in this excerpt Lawrence seems to say that giving is as important as taking, and that this is an "eternal" principle. It's also a moral position. It appears that he's captured by ambivalence, and it's fair to say that he's confused by it.

We know more about intuition and perception now than we did back when Lawrence wrote these letters, and we'll return to Lawrence in a moment. We move now to a different interpretation of what might be in "our blood" and "eternal" as it relates to making judgements.

"True north"

In *Principled-Centred Leadership*, Stephen R. Covey approaches leadership and decision-making by elaborating on the concept of "principles":

> Principles are not invented by us or by society; they are the laws of the universe that pertain to human relationships and human organisations. They are part of the human condition, consciousness and conscience. (Covey, 1992, p. 18)

The passion in what Lawrence calls "our blood" is absent here, replaced by a calm expression of "principles", but Covey agrees with Lawrence that they are universal and eternal and part of being human. So what are these principles, and where do they come from? If they are the "laws of the universe", and "part of the human condition", are we born with them already in our DNA as Lawrence suggests, or are other things separate from that at work here? Covey continues, invoking the moral primacy of the leadership frameworks we explored in Chapter 13.

> When managing in the wilderness of the changing times, a map is of limited worth. What's needed is a moral compass ... Principles are like a compass. A compass has a true north that is **objective and external**, that reflects natural laws or **principles**, as opposed to values that are subjective and internal. Because the compass represents the verities of life, we must develop our value system with deep respect for "true north" principles. (Covey, 1992, p. 94)

Covey elaborates on what his "principles" look like when acted out as "part of the human condition, consciousness and conscience":

> They don't change or shift. They provide "true north" direction to our lives when navigating the "streams" of our environments ... Principle-centred leadership is based on the reality that we cannot violate these natural laws with impunity. (Covey, 1992, pp. 18-19)

> *Principle-centred leadership is based on the reality that we cannot violate these natural laws with impunity.*

I think it's reasonable to conceptualise what Lawrence and Covey are talking about here as intuition: an understanding that includes but goes beyond the human dispositions of intellect and emotion, or the capabilities that evolve over many years to become "expert intuition". Both authors go further, invoking values and beliefs. Though one presents as passionate and emotive and the other appears calm and reasoned, are Lawrence and Covey essentially saying the same thing? Is Lawrence's reference to "blood" and "eternal" the same as Covey's reference to "the laws of the universe" which are "part of the human condition"? We need to note that Covey wrote from a religious standpoint as a Mormon, believing in a particular concept of divinity, which surely influences his understanding of where the "laws of the universe" come from. In part contrast, we know that Lawrence rejected organised religion but not a belief in God, stating that he was an agnostic, not prepared to claim an understanding of theology, allowing for doubt and ambiguity.

Notwithstanding these differences, both Lawrence and Covey seem to be saying that whatever intuition is, part of it is there either with us or waiting for us when we come into the world. It's universal, and it shows us the way to truth or "true north". It was there before the fire in the basement, before the chess players, and before that financial adviser made his investment decisions.

The long and winding road about decision-making that we've been travelling has now taken us into the territory of mystery and metaphysics. What are we to make of it?

Stay true to ourselves

Without being able to pin it down, we must accept that every time we're engaged in making a decision, intuition is there in all its complexity. Understand it as just another challenge in the age of ambiguity, but comfort yourself with the knowledge that it's not new: if Lawrence and Covey are right, it was there long before you and I walked along this road, and the most important thing is not to let it derail or immobilise your decision-making processes. Just accept that it's there and it's complicated.

It's not simple, but as we've already noted, decision-making is about the management of meaning: we can't avoid letting our intuition in; we just need to ensure that we're aware of the complexity and nuance it involves, put it in its place, and stay true to ourselves as we navigate our way through it.

Between the idea
And the reality ...

- *What do you make of the ways D. H. Lawrence and Stephen Covey conceptualise intuition? What is your intuition saying to you about their views?*

CHAPTER 21

Conflict avoidance, bias and noise

> "I sit and look out upon all the sorrows of the world,
> and upon all oppression and shame …
>
> All these – all the meanness and agony without end,
> I sitting, look out upon,
>
> See, hear, and am silent."
>
> – Walt Whitman

Conflict avoidance

Difficult decisions rarely involve a simple process to reach a solution; in fact it would be a concern if they did. Debate and conflict are not the same thing, but sometimes intense debate can merge into conflict when a complex issue is being addressed, especially if emotions are involved. Most of us enjoy debate but find conflict unpleasant. It gets mixed in with our mindscapes, our emotions and our intuition, and most of us will avoid it if we can. The problem is, historically and in organisational research, and in my own experience, conflict avoidance can ultimately result in greater conflict than when the issue first presented itself. That is a danger for the River Valley leadership team, because it may be that some level of conflict in the school community and even within the team is going to be inevitable in resolving the problem of Emily and her marijuana leaf.

Many organisational researchers and writers point out that it's normal for organisations to prefer harmony and agreement over dissent or conflict, and with effective leadership this is often achievable through discussion and negotiation. But there are times when conflict is inevitable, and trying to avoid it can lead to school leadership teams having surface agreement on a decision, but actual disagreement at a deeper level because some things were tacitly regarded by everyone as "undiscussables". But they're still there.

Back to Daniel Goleman, who addresses this tension through the concepts of *alignment* and *attunement* (Goleman, 2002). Alignment, he suggests, is essentially an intellectual exercise operating on the surface: people do things because that's expected of them, but they don't feel involved and their hearts are often not in it. Attunement, on the other hand, touches people's emotions as well as their intellect, and they feel motivated and committed because of the way the leadership has engaged them in the decision-making process. If there's alignment without attunement in a decision, especially if the issue is complex, Goleman suggests that problems are likely to occur when the decision rolls out into action, including confusion among the leadership team members themselves.

Kahneman, Siboney and Sunstein describe an example concerning a school's admissions process: one person reads an application file, evaluates it, and sends it with their rating to a second person, who also rates it. When a consultant suggested that it might be preferable not to provide the first reader's rating so as not to influence the second person's judgement, the principal explained that they used to do that, but there were so many disagreements that they moved to the current system. Surface agreement – alignment – is in place, but not necessarily attunement. The school is now treating conflict avoidance with the same level of importance as making the best decision (Kahneman et al., 2021).

It seems that gaining attunement was seen as too difficult and likely to involve conflict, so the school leadership decided to engage in a surface process of alignment. Ironically, if the process is challenged, which processes like school and college admissions often are, the surface agreement soon breaks down and the original decision is shown to be lacking in integrity. They will have to start over, address the issues that caused disagreement, and ultimately reach attunement or a compromise that comes close to it.

Cascades

Timur Kuran and Cass Sunstein have researched similar territory to this, sometimes relating it to conflict avoidance, among other things. They refer to what they call "availability cascades", explaining the concept as:

> ... a pervasive mental shortcut whereby the perceived likelihood of any given event is tied to the ease with which its occurrence can be brought to mind. Cognitive psychologists consider the availability heuristic to be a key determinant of individual judgement and perception. (Kuran & Sunstein, 1999, p. 2)

Kuran and Sunstein suggest that sometimes the experiences and insights that we have at the time of making a judgement or a decision may not be complete enough for us to make a balanced assessment of the issue. (You'll remember that's one of the mistakes I own up to in Chapter 8, when I look back at why some decisions went wrong in the past.) They suggest that the assessments we make are frequently based on "the ease with which we can think of relevant examples", and these untested assessments link into other untested assessments in a cascade that flows away from the core issues:

> *... the assessments we make are frequently based on "the ease with which we can think of relevant examples", and these untested assessments link into other untested assessments in a cascade that flows away from the core issues.*

> [They] generate availability cascades – social cascades, or simply cascades, through which expressed perceptions trigger chains of individual responses that make these perceptions appear increasingly plausible through their rising availability in public discourse ... The resulting mass delusions may last indefinitely and they may produce wasteful or even detrimental laws and policies ... Under the right conditions, many or most of the society's members, potentially even all, will end up with essentially identical beliefs, which may well be fanciful. (Kuran & Sunstein, 1999, p. 2)

This is what Judith Curry was alluding to regarding climate change in Chapter 8. Kahneman and colleagues cite three examples in the United States in the late 20th century when billions of dollars were spent by governments on issues that were generated by availability cascades which became the dominant narrative on an issue, only for the narrative to be subsequently found to be baseless, and ultimately discredited. It's a phenomenon with some similarities to what we've come to know as groupthink, but Kuran and Sunstein go further, analysing availability cascades into two types, both directly related to decision-making:

Information cascades occur when people knowingly or unknowingly have incomplete information on a particular issue, and choose to defer to the overt beliefs of other people, perhaps through indifference, diffidence, emotion, delegated authority, or some combination of these. Because some believe it, and perhaps express opinions persuasively or loudly, others decide to believe it or at least accept it, then others, causing a cascade effect flowing throughout a community. It becomes the "truth": the dominant narrative.

Reputational cascades don't happen because people defer their thinking to others on an issue through lack of information, conflict avoidance or diffidence; they happen through political expediency. People speak and act as if they support a particular cause because of its ideological base, or they seek to find favour with what might appear to be a dominant social view. The aim is for people to earn approval or avoid censure, irrespective of their own personal thoughts on the issue. As more and more people join in, the cascade grows, moving from a dominant narrative to becoming *the* dominant narrative, irrespective of its actual veracity.

Awareness

These two types of availability cascades are not necessarily mutually exclusive, and can reinforce each other to form a joint snowball effect: a powerful and often fast-flowing cascade that can quickly move a decision-making process away from the core issues and into detours that result in serious errors of judgement. The good news is that leaders are usually aware that they are vulnerable to these cascade effects, and if they are tempted to defer to the views of others for one or more of the reasons above, they can decide to rise above them or knowingly go ahead with one or both in their decision-making.

The bad news is that a wrong – indeed a disastrous – decision can result from knowingly or unknowingly succumbing to an availability cascade. As we noted earlier, a key element in complex decision-making is self-awareness: being aware that this is what we are doing, and why; also being aware of the possible consequences of doing so, especially if the evidence base for the narrative is untested, or it creates intuitive tension with our personal mindscapes or pits our intellect against our emotions.

This is complicated stuff, not to be taken lightly. Quick, decisive decision-making won't cut it: that's the way to an availability cascade with all the dangers accompanying it. The key is full awareness of the issue along with self-awareness, and that is often slow to clarify and reveal itself to us. So … sleep on it. And would it be tedious if I again asked you to remind yourself who won that race?

The signal, the noise, and bias

> Wherever there is judgement there is noise – and more of it than you think. (Kahneman et al., 2021)

In his work on prediction, Nate Silver uses the terms "signal" and "noise" (Silver, 2012). In Chapter 8, I listed some of the reasons my leadership team and I had got a decision wrong; one was that we gave too much importance to something that proved to be not important: it was a distraction and it influenced our decision far more than it should have. That's what Silver refers to as "noise", and he points out the ways it can divert our decision-making away from the core issue, the "signal".

Silver largely presents noise as visible and able to be taken into account in making judgements and decisions as long as we see it for what it is. Kahneman, Siboney and Sunstein develop the concept further, pointing out the potential impact of noise when decision-makers are not aware that it's there. They suggest that noise differs from bias because we are often – though not always – aware of bias in our thinking and decision-making. Noise, on the other hand, can sneak its way into our decisions without our awareness. And unlike bias, it operates quite separately in our minds from the issue at hand, but can seriously impact our decisions without our realising it.

Kahneman and his colleagues define noise as "undesirable variability in judgements of the same problem", differentiating it from bias (Kahneman et al., 2021). Bias is perhaps the easier concept, because it has a common meaning, and we can often identify if we're experiencing it when making decisions, even if we need external advice to recognise it. It's there in all of us, speaking to us through our gut feelings, impacting on our judgements. The impact isn't such a problem if we're aware that it's there in our mindscapes, and we either affirm it for a particular decision, modify it or reject it. It only becomes a problem when we're not aware of it or pretend it's not there when we sense that it is.

15 years or 30 days?

Noise is dangerous because it has been shown to have a major impact on people's decision-making, sometimes in ways that will take your breath away. Let's draw out its relevance to decision-making in a way that is simple but not simplistic.

> *Noise is dangerous because it has been shown to have a major impact on people's decision-making, sometimes in ways that will take your breath away.*

Kahneman and colleagues conducted research on the level of consistency in American judges' sentencing of people without previous convictions who had been convicted of the same crime. They have then drawn from similar research in other western countries. Their findings are consistent, astonishing and frightening. One example: In 1973 two men without previous convictions were convicted of trying to cash counterfeit cheques, one for $58.40 and the other for $35.20. The first man was sentenced to 15 **years**, and the second to 30 **days**. An independent judge researched these and other decisions by judges. He found that the sentence imposed depended less on the crime or the individual defendant, and more on the individual views and biases of the individual judges – and on noise. The same defendant in the same case could receive widely differing sentences depending on which judge was hearing the case, and when, and where it was being heard.

Other researchers conducted similar investigations in the later 1970s and early 1980s, and all revealed examples of the same wild differences in sentencing by judges among similar cases. In 1984 Congress passed legislation requiring judges to follow a mandated set of guidelines in sentencing, and in the following years the discrepancies decreased significantly. Some judges objected to what they saw as an invasion of their professional discretionary powers and in 2005, after lobbying by the judges on a technical issue, the United States Supreme Court struck down the legislation that created the mandatory guidelines. Studies since 2005 indicate a return to the inconsistencies that characterised the situation prior to the establishing of the guidelines. When judges allow noise into their decisions, the integrity of a country's legal system comes into question.

The thing is, they were probably unaware that it was there: noise just sneaks in under the radar and does its work.

If that is concerning, now it gets frightening. Drawing from multiple studies of millions of judgements including in the United States and France, Kahneman and colleagues offer further examples of the impact noise can have on a sentencing decision. Some of the trends identified in the research:

- Judges are more lenient at the start of the day than at the end.
- When the local football team loses a game on the weekend, judges are harsher on Monday than when the team wins, continuing to a lesser extent during the week.
- Judges are more lenient if sentencing on the defendant's or the judge's birthday.
- A study of 207,000 immigration decisions by courts in France showed that if it is hot outside on the day of the hearing, judges are statistically less likely to grant asylum than on days when it is cool.

The researchers offer similar examples of noise influencing executives' decision-making in the corporate world. It's a universal problem, and these examples make clear how noise differs from bias. Bias may be playing a part, but it's usually consistent: noise appears unconsciously and randomly, so much so that the decision-makers are unaware of its influence – and as we can see, that influence can be significant.

That's the danger of noise. We might be aware that those factors are there, but we don't realise they are impacting significantly on our cognitive processing, and therefore on our decision-making. Neither our emotions nor intuition pick them up, so unlike with bias, we can't identify them in our mindscapes. And they're neither intellectual nor emotional: they're just there, every time we engage in decision-making, in "the wildness lying in wait".

What are we to do we do with all this?

We've engaged in a lengthy and wide-ranging discussion that has ranged through intuition, emotion, bias, the signal, and noise. You may be wondering if we're over-complicating things. Is it really necessary to go into all this nuance and complexity when all you're interested in is making a good decision? Shouldn't we just get on with it? Surely it's just like driving a car. After all, you can be an expert driver without understanding the complexity of how a modern combustion or electric engine works. Aren't we essentially talking about the same thing?

I think there's a difference. A motor vehicle is a machine, and if there's a problem we can usually fix it because its workings are predictable and quantifiable. Intuition, bias, the signal and noise are neither of these, because as we've discussed, the human mind is not a machine. That's why the world's most capable and respected researchers, writers and thinkers still can't agree on what this thing we call intuition actually is, or where it comes from. It's a tricky, non-material phenomenon, involving past experience, emotions, intellect, values, and depending on your beliefs, it may even have a numinous dimension. And it kicks in at the very beginning of a decision-making process, so it can lead to "conclusion bias" or "substitution bias" (Kahneman et al., 2021), where we make a decision without deeper analysis of quantitative and qualitative data or context over time, and without our tortoise mind having a chance to balance our hare brain. Or perhaps we've compounded that intuitive decision by also succumbing to an availability cascade, resulting in "conclusion bias", drawing only from data that support our "confirmation bias", and ignoring any that don't. That combination is danger territory for a school or system leader making decisions about complex issues that affect the workings of the organisation. Again, don't be daunted by it, just be aware that it's there, and take care as you think a decision through.

*

I hope that's got you thinking, because it's all relevant to the quality and effectiveness of your leadership, and therefore your decisions. Where does it lead us in its implications for when this devilish brew kicks in, as it surely will every time you're engaged in decision-making? The thing is, when it comes to the really tough decisions – especially those that have an emotional dimension and where you find yourself well and truly immersed in the age of ambiguity – I can say from experience that there, still, beneath it all, are your mindscapes: your values and beliefs, guiding how you see the world. So too is your "expert intuition", with warning signs cautioning you based on previous experiences. That's self-awareness, and above all it implies being true to yourself. You're balancing the emotional component of your intuition against more analytical thinking, and sometimes moderating it and leaning to the analytical, keeping in mind that undetected noise will almost certainly be trying to influence your thinking too. And yet again, here's where the wildness is lying in wait: if one part of your intuition is pushing against that balance and you stick only with your feelings in the face of credible evidence pushing back, you'll experience a paradox: the other components of your intuition, including the expert part, will tell you later that you got that decision wrong. And this time your intuition will be right.

The key learning from all this complexity is to be aware that when making a decision intuition, emotion, bias and noise are always there, but so is the signal. We need to keep our antennae tuned for each, especially for the signal – the core of the issue – as it may not be obvious at first glance. What appear to be minor and unrelated factors might well be impacting our thinking in ways that are far from minor. Just be aware of it.

And now, amid all this, there's one more thing, and it should bring you some peace of mind – if you're humble enough to heed it. In their classic work, *Good to Great* (2001), Jim Collins and his research team set out to find if organisations that were long-term high performers had common characteristics. They found that those organisations did indeed have some commonality, one feature being the nature of their chief executive officers. In every high-performing organisation, the CEOs exhibited two deeply held and consistently practised qualities. The first the researchers called *professional will* – a passion for the work the organisation is engaged in. No surprise there, but there was with the second quality: *humility*. Every one of them approached their work, including the people working with them, with humility. And that applied to their decision-making. They never had a quick fix. None of them were charismatic, and none of them exhibited the hubris that characterised the judges who saw themselves as above being required to act within consistent guidelines. Those CEOs sometimes appeared indecisive, but they weren't; they were exercising their own versions of *dadirri*.

So just having the ability to be humble and accept the complexity and uncertainty that characterises difficult decisions is likely to help in your decision-making when you're dealing with complexity. If you can practise it you'll be in good company: actually "great" company.

*

I'm confident that we've drawn together enough information and advice from researchers and thinkers about intuition, emotion, availability cascades, bias and noise to draw some conclusions about how they can impact on our judgements. Intuition is usually a positive guide in decision-making – but that's the point: it's a guide, and it's not infallible. The way forward is to be careful before acting on it, but don't try to dismiss it. It's too powerful, and you won't be able to dismiss it even if you try. Pause on it, hear what it's saying to you, and let it quietly percolate within your mindscapes, along with your leadership framework and your other decision-making strategies. Don't be daunted by it: that's why I've written this book.

Ultimately, your self-awareness will see you through, along with a healthy dose of humility. They will sift through the complexity, discern among the nuance, ambivalence and ambiguity, and very likely guide your thinking through to the best decision. You'll sense it rather than know it. Don't let the complexity immobilise you. Take a deep breath, quietly remind yourself that you know this is difficult territory, and you understand it. Remember, you're clear about your mindscapes, your tortoise mind is quietly and steadily processing it, and you have the final decision in hand because you know how this works: you know who ultimately wins that race irrespective of how many times you read the story.

To speak or not to speak ...

A final thought to wrap up this chapter: Sometimes your thinking will bring you face to face with an availability cascade that has become the dominant narrative for an issue, but on reflection you've decided it's wrong. Do you speak out, or do you avoid potential conflict by staying silent? Offering your view in that situation is hard and you may not initially be thanked for it; indeed, in today's world you may be cancelled for it. But here are some more words from W. B. Yeats, from the same poem we looked at in Chapter 4. Describing the times he found himself living in, Yeats wrote:

> The best lack all conviction, while the worst
> Are full of passionate intensity.

In hindsight we can see that this was certainly the case in the years between the two World Wars. Powerful availability cascades were at work, particularly in Germany, Italy and Japan, and so was bias, playing on people's emotions, generating ideas and feelings that drew millions into dominant narratives that shook the world to its foundations. I don't believe that history literally repeats itself, but some things, including availability cascades, bias and noise leading to dominant but false narratives, do recur, as captured so powerfully in Yeats's words.

*

So let's come back to Pete Seeger's question from the 1960s, because he saw that what was happening then had happened before, and on each occasion it had ended very badly. So his question stands: "When will they ever learn?" (And should that "they" perhaps be a "we"?) Maybe when "the best" are able to summon up the courage and conviction to speak in the face of the "passionate intensity" of a questionable narrative? That narrative may well be a false availability cascade, but if you speak there may be a personal cost, as there was for J. Robert Oppenheimer. And so again we face the tension between the idea and the reality. It's always there, and only you can make the call.

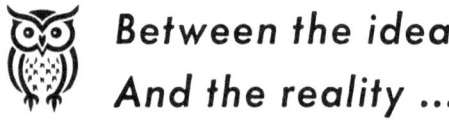

Between the idea
And the reality …

- *Has there been a time when you have let conflict avoidance interfere with making the right decision? Most leaders have at some point. Did you learn from it?*
- *Can you think of a time when you knowingly or unknowingly subscribed to an availability cascade? How did it work out?*
- *Where does this collection of research and thinking about intuition, emotion, conflict avoidance, availability cascades, bias, the signal and noise fit with your leadership framework? Can you simplify it without making it simplistic, and fit it into the mindscapes that guide your decision-making?*
- *In* Blink *(2005) Malcolm Gladwell warns against over-thinking complex issues, suggesting that our intuition will guide us correctly even if we can't explain why, and that introspection is more likely to confuse us in making decisions. Have I perhaps "overthought" things over the last four chapters?*

CHAPTER 22

To know the place for the first time

> "We shall not cease from exploration
> And the end of all our exploring
> Will be to arrive where we started
> And know the place for the first time."
> – T. S. Eliot

So, after the journey we've taken through the previous chapters, where have we arrived? It's simple, but not simplistic. As a school leader, every time you sit down, stand, walk, even sleep when deliberating over a decision, everything in the previous chapters is in play. Even the most straight-forward decision can turn out to be not so straight-forward, because, like Craig Foster in *My Octopus Teacher*, you can't see beneath the surface of what you're dealing with unless you develop the capacity to go there. Remember the rats of Hanoi. Add to that another layer – the uncertainty and complexity of the age of ambiguity – and it's clear that there's much to think about and make sense of.

My point is, we can make sense of it if we think about it, but it's the kind of thinking that takes patience and preparation. That's where we've arrived at after walking that long and winding road, and it's brought us back to the letter writer in the prologue: Do we hit the ground running, or hit the ground thinking? Do we take the time to learn how to free-dive so we can see the milieu of what's below the surface, or do we skate along on the surface assuming that's all there is? Do we encounter a problem and like the Peruvian health officials move quickly to a structural decision, or do we pause before acting, and dig deeper looking for any cultural artefacts that might lie at the heart of the problem?

Back to the future?

We've walked together through country characterised by research, reflection and experience, processing it through our own unique mindscapes. We've paused at various places along the way to absorb the learnings the various sojourns have offered us as decision-makers.

Have you sensed along the way that sometimes we might be moving through places you've been before? That it wasn't all new or unknown territory? That much of what we have encountered along the way was already there in your head, but you hadn't paused long enough to find the words, or to fully process the concepts into firm ideas? And in your decision-making, have you sometimes had that feeling of nausea described by Jean-Paul Sartre in Chapter 4, without understanding why it's there? Could it be that Stephen Covey's "true north" may not be straight ahead somewhere over the horizon, but actually closer to home and you've been there before? Maybe that's because "wherever you go, there you are". Perhaps your mindscapes have changed or moderated during the journey, or perhaps they're intact. Wherever you are at this point, I hope they're clearer in your mind and at a broader and deeper level than they were before you started reading; and I hope that you're more confident about their place in your decision-making, and indeed, in your leadership.

I'm also hopeful enough to suggest that along the way you've become more confident in who you are: that you're the same person as the one who began the journey, but perhaps more aware and familiar with that person now – wiser, seeing greater meaning in what you do, and feeling more at peace with the way it fits with your leadership and decision-making amid the contesting pressures of the age of ambiguity. In a sense, maybe you are coming full circle, "knowing the place for the first time"?

*

The River Valley High leadership team are now in the final stages of their process, and they're close to making a decision. Before we join them, it's important to take a moment and review the journey, and the places we've encountered along the way.

- Like Craig Foster free-diving in *My Octopus Teacher*, we've observed and reflected on the landscape, both on the surface and beneath it. We've been on many thinking expeditions, delving into research and experience, not actively canvassing solutions and answers, but first making sense of things by seeking meaning and wisdom. At the same time, having done that, it's very likely the solutions will come more easily now. Decision-making in the age of ambiguity will always be hard, but this kind of leadership thinking comes before the answers and solutions; it's actually paving the way for them.
- Having walked this far beside you, I'm confident the decisions you'll come up with will be more meaningful and effective than any "off-the-shelf" blueprints offered from outside your own unique context, or by charismatic action-oriented leaders you might see around you. Aesop is speaking to you from Ancient Athens, reassuring you that you're getting it right.
- Along the way, we've walked with researchers, educators, historians, storytellers, poets, an artist, novelists, psychologists, scientists, musicians, songwriters and philosophers, some of whom include Australia's First People. We've looked a long way back, and in varying ways we've heard a continuing story: uncertainty, anxiety, change, complexity and nuance characterise today's world; but this is not something unique to today. It's been part of the human experience from as far back as we are able to see, and dwells as much in our minds and hearts as it does in our external environment. These features have evolved and mutated over the years, sometimes slowly, sometimes rapidly, and they manifest themselves differently now. And they are a necessary part of our ability to continue to evolve as human beings, little by little building our resilience and making things a little better.
- We've taken some key insights from Tom Sergiovanni, including his two "worlds" and the idea of a school having a "covenant".
- We've encountered challenging understandings of "reality" and "truth", pondering Peter Drucker's claim that "reality never stands still for long". To affirm our own realities and truths, we've explored our *mindscapes* or *mental models*.
- We've walked through the confusing landscape of chaos theory, making sense of it by drawing from Peter Senge's fifth discipline of *systems thinking*, understanding and accepting that everything is connected whether we can see the connections or not. Understanding this and making sense of it without becoming immobilised in our

- decision-making is one of the leadership capabilities we've been developing along the way.
- We've walked in the land of metaphor, drawing from it increasingly throughout the journey in order to clarify what it is we're trying to get at: finding a way through, simplifying while not being simplistic. And we'll go further into that when we return to River Valley High.
- Henry Mintzberg met us at one point to assert that there is too much strategic planning and not enough strategic thinking; and Karl Weick offered insight and wisdom through the concept of loosely-coupled systems, especially as it applies to schools and education systems.
- We met up with the River Valley High School leadership team and colleagues walking the same road, deep in discussion and grappling with a problem they are struggling to make sense of. We paused to take in their issue, then moved on, promising to reflect on their problem and join them again further down the road.
- We paused to take some time for contemplation, thinking about "the silence in our mind": *dadirri* from Australia's First People; "slow thinking" from a cognitive scientist; and Aesop's fable about the hare and the tortoise, gifting us with the simple but not simplistic concept of the hare brain and tortoise mind and the wisdom of "sleeping on it".
- We've stopped in on the Rijksmuseum in Amsterdam to take in the art of Pieter de Hooch, attended a jazz concert, and drawn some wisdom from Jacob Collier, Count Basie and Miles Davis. We've drawn from the poetry of T. S. Eliot, and taken a subtle but harsh learning about the power of culture from a village in the foothills of the Andes.
- As we continued along the way, we were faced with the ancient question – *Why are we here?* – with ideas from William Shakespeare among others including Michael Fullan, Simon Sinek and Mike Edwards, the latter three offering leadership frameworks for decision-making: all circular, all grounded in moral purpose, saying to us, "You must be able to address that question and be able to say with confidence, "This is why we're here".
- We caught up with Frank Crowther from the University of Southern Queensland, and John MacBeath from Cambridge, to take in their concept of leadership as going beyond positional status, and in fact dwelling in all areas of the school, eager to contribute, waiting to be invited into our decision-making processes.
- We walked a lengthy section of the journey through the territory of school culture, taking in landscapes ranging from far-reaching vision

through to relationships and everyday courtesies, all of which go to make up the "soul" of the organisation. During our walk through culture territory we followed many signposts, with three in particular pointing us toward the important places of *hope, belief* and *trust*.

- We looked at three examples of military structures guided not by command but by culture.
- We spent time on three linked insights: the way the Pygmalion effect can impact on young people's development, the Danish principle of *dannelse*, and Carol Dweck's two mindsets.
- We took a lengthy detour to explore the extraordinarily complex and elusive concepts of intuition, bias and noise, seeking to distil them into understandings that are simple but not simplistic, emphasising the need for self-awareness in handling these tricky artefacts of the mind which can be both enlightening and deceptive in our decision-making.

And here we are, with learnings about decision-making in the age of ambiguity, with, I hope, a deeper understanding of how complex and nuanced that whole area is. At the beginning, early in our walk, I said to you that we were looking to develop two particular capabilities to guide us in our judgements: *meaning* and *wisdom*, that we would be focusing on people ahead of systems and structures, and that we would be engaging in *the management of meaning*: for ourselves, and for those we aspire to lead.

Before we rejoin the River Valley High leadership team, we need to explore a device often used by poets, novelists, politicians and others who use words to strengthen and deepen what they're trying to say. Thanks to some insightful thinking and research, we know that leaders can also use it to deepen their understanding when making difficult decisions. We're talking about *metaphor*, and it will be instrumental in the way the River Valley problem-solvers wrap up their decision.

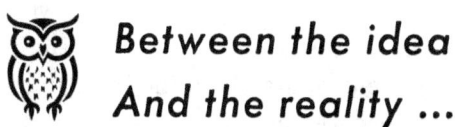

Between the idea
And the reality ...

- *Is there one particular stop along the long and winding road that has made a more significant impact on your thinking than any of the others? Or more than one? Pause here and jot down a few thoughts about why, and how it (they) might influence your decision-making processes.*

CHAPTER 23

The power of metaphor

> "Metaphors provide 'picture words' that consolidate complex ideas into a single, understandable whole".
> – Terrence Deal and Kent Peterson

> "The use of metaphor implies **a way of thinking** and **a way of seeing** that pervades how we understand our world generally ... By using different metaphors to understand the complex and paradoxical character of organisational life, we are able to manage and design organisations in ways that we may not have thought possible before".
> – Gareth Morgan

In Chapter 15 we explored Sergiovanni's concepts of the lifeworld and the systemsworld. Researchers and thinkers like Gareth Morgan, Lee Bolman and Terrence Deal take this conceptualising further. In *Reframing Organisations*, Bolman and Deal deploy metaphor to delve deeper into the life of organisations in a complex world. They offer strategies that help clarify and identify the dynamics of how an organisation works, especially when an important decision has to be made.

Reframing

The River Valley leadership team and their colleagues are now at "the pointy end" of pushing toward a solution to the problem posed by Emily's marijuana leaf. They know they need to cover multiple perspectives, and in order to simplify and analyse what they are dealing with, they have opted to use Bolman and Deal's strategy of *reframing*. They have done this before, and they know that while it isn't a blueprint for a solution, the reframing strategy assists them to cover all the bases; they are unlikely to miss something important.

Reframing takes four differing but integrated perspectives on the same issue, allocating a metaphor to each perspective and delving into the issue at hand with each one. The framework is grounded in the power of metaphor to analyse and clarify complex issues. Bolman and Deal suggest that metaphors can not only make clear intellectually what we were sensing intuitively but were unable to express, but also enable us to tap into senses and feelings that include but go beyond the intellectual.

*

Read this sentence describing a scene:

> There was a strong wind blowing clouds across the moon, which shone on the road as the highwayman rode up to the inn.

Now read the opening lines of Alfred Noyes's poem "The Highwayman", describing the same scene:

> The wind was a torrent of darkness among the gusty trees.
>
> The moon was a ghostly galleon tossed upon cloudy seas.
>
> The road was a ribbon of moonlight over the purple moor,
>
> And the highwayman came riding
>
> Riding, riding,
>
> The highwayman came riding
>
> Up to the old inn door.

Two descriptions of the same scene. One clinically describes the scene in plain words. What more could you want? Well, in a different context, perhaps this: Alfred Noyes has created an atmosphere using evocative metaphors and rhythms to touch our senses as well as our intellect. It's a leading question, of course, but which of the two pieces stimulates your mind more? That's a hint at the power of metaphor, and we're now taking it into the realm of leadership and decision-making.

Four frames

Bolman and Deal tap this power through their four "frames" for organisations: the *factory* (structural), the *family* (human resource), the *jungle* (political), and the temple (*symbolic*). It's like looking through the window frames of a four-walled room, with people working inside. Each window reveals a different view of the same room and the same people working on the same thing. As we move from window to window, we see changes, and with it the language and also the meaning changes. Each frame is a metaphor for the organisation, capturing different perspectives with different words. We're looking at the same thing through the same eyes each time, but through a different window, seeing it from a different perspective.

> *We're looking at the same thing through the same eyes each time, but through a different window, seeing it from a different perspective.*

It's a simple framework, but it's far from simplistic. Indeed, the further you develop it, the more it reveals deep understanding of what lies undetected beneath the surface in all organisations, especially schools. And the four frames are not discrete: they interact with one another in ways that take some time to fully understand and synthesise: systems thinking is clearly at work here, as it always is.

It's important to understand that the framework won't provide our leadership team with a decision. What it will do, though, is stimulate their thinking in ways that will help them to engage in the management of meaning, uncovering nuance and complexity, and gleaning the information they will need in order to make a balanced decision. After applying and discussing how the four metaphors apply to the issue being addressed, there are choices to be made as the decision-makers synthesise and refine what they have found through their mindscapes and leadership framework.

They've learnt some things along the way, especially that there are some things you can control and some you can't; some you can influence and some you can't; some you can neither control nor influence; and they've learnt that some things are there even though you can't see them, but just being aware that they're there and knowing their potential to influence your thinking is helpful in avoiding distractions or becoming immobilised.

The first frame: the factory

The factory metaphor focuses on the school's structures, systems, rules, policies and norms. When this frame is optimal the school is functioning as "a well-oiled machine": teachers and students are all on time for class, everyone is on time for scheduled meetings, lessons are always well prepared, students have all done their homework and work quietly in class, engaged in the lesson. Teachers have all the resources they need. There are no behaviour problems, everyone interprets policies in the same way, there are no silos across faculties and subject disciplines, there are no parent complaints, everyone meets deadlines, there is no bullying or vandalism, all students behave well in public including how they present themselves, and all students are achieving strong academic results.

That's fanciful, of course, but it lays out the scope of this frame and reminds us that as long as people are involved the idea will be different from the reality. Constant and consistent maintenance understood by everyone is the key to this frame, just as it is in a real factory. And the language is quite specific: *alignment, efficiency, policies, compliance, control, programs, machines, technology, maintenance, products, outcomes, risk management, costs, delivery, profit and loss, bottom line, balance sheet, results,* and so on. A leading question: Which of Sergiovanni's worlds are we in here?

For any organisation to be working well, including a school, the factory frame needs to be functioning effectively because it impacts on the other three frames. Based on their research, the authors reveal that many organisational leaders – including in schools – operate primarily through the factory frame, including in their interactions with people. This means they're likely to miss much of the organic life of the organisation, most of which revolves around people and relationships, not technology, systems and structures. That one-dimensional perspective can have a major impact on the effectiveness of the organisation, even leading at times to what some researchers have called "organisational drift", where in their decision-making even the leadership can lose sight of why we are here.

The second frame: the family

> It was a town of red brick that would have been red if the smoke and ashes had allowed it; but as matters stood it was a town of unnatural red and black like the painted face of a savage … [T]here was a rattling and a trembling all day long, where the piston of the steam engine worked monotonously up and down like the head of an elephant in a state of melancholy madness.
>
> It contained several large streets all very like one another, and many more streets still more like one another, inhabited by people equally like one another, who all went in and out at the same hours, with the same sound upon the same pavements, to do the same work, and to whom every day was the same as yesterday and tomorrow, and every year the counterpart of the last and the next. (Dickens, 2008, p. 26)

Those are the words of Charles Dickens in his novel *Hard Times*, published in 1854. It was a time when the industrial revolution in northern England was at its most heartless and soulless, captured so evocatively in Dickens's words. Indeed, through words such as these, Dickens was among the first to point to the industrial revolution's dehumanising effects on ordinary people in the mid and late 19th century. He was read widely, and his work tapped the consciences of politicians who gradually began to see the need to legislate for change. It would take longer for business leaders to see that it also had relevance to the effectiveness of their organisations, and even later for educational leaders to see it. Some still don't.

Dickens's agenda was mostly humane, highlighting the damaging social impact of treating people like the cogs of machines in a factory. It wasn't until well into the 20th century that researchers and enlightened business leaders began to understand that the people in an organisation are actually more than cogs in a production line. Psychologists, researchers and other writers and thinkers have pursued this into the 21st century, to a point where irrespective of whether we're talking about education or manufacturing or any other enterprise, the human life of organisations has come to be seen as its most important element. That's where the family metaphor comes in. Those researchers were looking through a different frame from that of the factory. They were seeing the organisation as a human entity, with important implications for leadership and decision-making.

The language and the assumptions about a school change when viewed through this frame, acknowledging the importance of human needs as well as those of the organisation: people and organisations have mutual needs, with organisations needing ideas, commitment and talent, and people needing careers, satisfaction and fulfilment through their work. That means both individual satisfaction and organisational effectiveness depend heavily on the quality of interpersonal relations in the school, and when the organisation is viewed through this frame, the language changes to words like *relationships, trust, respect, care, resilience, empathy, persistence, values, beliefs, emotional intelligence, attunement, support, potential*, and even *love*; and as we've noted, the language influences the thinking.

Another leading question: Which of Sergiovanni's worlds are we in here?

The third frame: the jungle

In December 2007 Pakistan's president, Benazir Bhutto, was asked in an interview whether she enjoyed having power. Her response:

> Power has made me suffer too much. In reality I'm ambivalent about it. It interests me because it makes it possible to change things. But it's left me with a bitter taste. (Bhutto in Bolman & Deal, 2013, p. 183)

The jungle metaphor is about power. It represents the political dimension of organisational life, and Benazir Bhutto's ambivalence is common for today's organisational leaders. It's about competing aspirations and expectations that can range across resourcing, industrial relations, and other structural issues. It's also about people's differing understandings of reality, and it reaches into the heart of why we are here. It links strongly with the family metaphor, because it's also about people and the vagaries of being human; that means it's an integral and dynamic player in every decision made by school leaders, ranging from a decision at a staff meeting about student behaviour through to a strategic decision about the future of the school. Or, as in Benazir Bhutto's case, to the future direction of a nation. And for her, it was a bitter taste indeed. She was assassinated a few days after that interview.

I think most school leaders would agree that the political frame is usually the most unpleasant and difficult of the four metaphors, because it often involves disagreement, and sometimes conflict. Nevertheless, despite the unpleasantness, you have to go there and encourage people with competing views to openly place them on the table, safe in the understanding that they will be treated with respect by the leadership and by their colleagues. When the issues aren't on the table, they're still alive and active, and they won't go away. They will surface informally in the carpark, the canteen, the pub on a Friday afternoon, or the local supermarket, generating all kinds of angst and dissatisfaction, much of it happening beneath the surface. And as with the other frames, the language changes: *alignment, competitors, competitive advantage, strategy, company, sustainability, advocacy, defensiveness, equity, inclusion, diversity* ... every one of them susceptible to ambiguity in interpretation.

Where does this frame fit in Sergiovanni's "worlds"? (That may not be so easy to answer.)

I found the need for openness in decision-making to be important, and when people felt they had been heard and genuinely listened to, they were usually satisfied. The work of Everett Rogers, whom we visited in Chapter 11, is especially helpful about this, and I found his insights to be affirmed on every occasion that a challenging issue was on the table. Rogers explains how people in an organisation will behave when a decision that involves changes in routine or behaviour is being implemented. There will be a bell-shaped curve rising from a small number of "innovators" through "early adopters" to an "early majority", then descending through a "late majority" to a small number of "laggards" (Rogers, 2003).

Affording the "laggards" the same respect as "innovators" and "early adopters" might be difficult, but we've seen how powerful respect and trust are in leading a school, and how important the principal's role is in it. Also, the terms Rogers uses to describe the ways people respond to issues are not personal labels: a laggard in one case may well be an innovator in another. I agree that the jungle is the most unpleasant and challenging area of decision-making, but if you're able to deploy your emotional intelligence in ways that preserve people's dignity and self-respect, the result can be surprisingly rewarding. The soft stuff really is the hard stuff.

The fourth frame: the temple or cathedral

When viewed through this frame, a school takes on deeper meaning. Like a temple or a cathedral, it can become almost a "hallowed" place: an expression of human aspirations and beliefs, "a monument to hope, and faith in human possibility" (Bolman & Deal, 2013, p. 403). We're on the same ground as Sergiovanni's covenant in Chapter 14: an agreed culture that has a deep, almost sacred nature to it. That's the frame we're in here, and it's at work whether we like it or not, mixing with the other three.

People come to temples or cathedrals to hear deep messages – to find meaning, purpose, hope, inspiration and security amid the complexities and anxieties of the world. This frame can include organised religion, but it goes beyond that to a sense of something spiritual, beyond the material world, that people hope for, perhaps even need, from their school. In some ways this frame is the opposite of the factory frame; yet it's important to accept that both are there every day, along with the other two frames, all important, integral players impacting on every decision.

When Hedley Beare suggested that schools are now people's main communities, this is what he was alluding to. I've come to understand that he was right, and it makes this frame particularly important for school leaders. And the language? We hear words like *faith, hope, sustenance, spiritual, compassion, soul, peace, grace, love, reflection, dedication, transcendence, belief,* and often, *life,* all again subject to ambiguity and interpretation, and all deeply human concepts.

Understanding the role of this metaphor in the life of the school is one of the places the long and winding road of this journey has led us to. As we've noted, it's sobering that many leaders and managers are unconsciously working from one, perhaps two of the frames at the most, with the factory metaphor the most prominent. Given all that we now know about the human factor in the performance of all organisations, it won't surprise you to learn that the authors also found those organisations were neither happy nor productive places.

We'll return to the four frames soon. The River Valley team are applying them to their thinking as they close in on their decision; and they're about to tap into some wisdom from an American presidential speech-writer in the 1980s.

What do we want it to do?

Peggy Noonan was President Ronald Reagan's main speech-writer. She explains how when the president approached her to talk about an important speech, he usually began with what he wanted to say. She always stopped him and asked, "What do you want this speech to **do**? What is its job?" (Noonan 1998; author's emphasis) . Only after this was thought about, discussed and answered by the president did they turn to what he wanted to say. The River Valley leadership team saw the wisdom in Noonan's strategy some time back, and have adapted it to their decision-making: *What do we want this decision to do? What is its job?*

That's where the team are going now. Responses begin to flow, some come quickly, others take longer to surface:

- We want it to be both strong and compassionate.
- It has to go deeper than a structural solution. There's a cultural dimension and we need to build it into the solution.

- We want it to be accepted by the great majority of the school community.
- We want it to show our leadership is sincere and authentic. No clichés, no bureaucratic weasel words, no avoiding a tough decision if that's what's needed.
- We want the decision to present this as a learning experience more than a punitive exercise.
- We want it to tell a positive story.
- We want Emily to face consequences, but we want her to go forward, not backward from this.
- We want it to show that River Valley High is not seen as soft on illegal drugs, or as having a "drug problem".

Perhaps you've observed that they're engaging in the management of meaning?

A lively conversation ensues, and they reach an agreed answer to Peggy Noonan's question:

> We want our decision to show that this school is compassionate toward its students and strong on illegal drugs.

That meets with approval around the table, and the team members sense a quiet shared confidence that they can do this. They are clear about what they want the decision to do, and that's a strong start.

The "delicate balances"

The conversation now ranges through questions, comments, assertions, hypotheticals (what if …), challenges, intellect, intuition, emotion and bemusement, to name some. There are no non-discussables, and trust and respect underpin the process.

They begin to flesh out the factory frame.

- The school must keep running smoothly. We can't let this dominate the agenda. We'll dig deep, but we can't take too long or the rumour mill will get away from us.
- We have a policy for this. We thought it through and we were careful and consultative in wording it. We must have the confidence to keep faith with it.

- There need to be relevant consequences so Emily and the school community understand that we see this as a serious matter.
- Some people are telling us we should just expel her and get the message out that we're strong on drugs, and get on with life.
- We're also dealing with the legal principle of duty of care, and we need to have that covered.

Some things are affirmed fairly quickly, including one big one: they agree that Emily will not be expelled. They return to their understanding that the decision should have a moral purpose, and they agree that they have identified this in their answer to Peggy Noonan's question. They informally personalise it to say they want their leadership to be seen as both compassionate and strong.

They move on and stretch out on the family frame:

- While this is about the credibility of the school's policies, it's also about Emily's wellbeing.
- It's not just Emily's wellbeing. We have to ensure the safety of all students at the school by eliminating illegal drugs from the campus, and continuing the educative process.
- Show compassion. She's young and she's made a mistake. We often say to the students that we see mistakes as learning opportunities. We have to walk the talk.
- Emily is still the "becoming person", so how do we keep faith with that in this situation?
- We're always consultative in our decision-making. That needs to apply here, and be seen to apply. We've worked hard over the years to establish our integrity in decision-making. People need to trust us to get it right.

They agree on another big decision: the first two dot points above are the key principles. They are perhaps the basis of the narrative to explain the decision. It's about balance, which is an overt fundamental principle in the school's culture.

Now for the jungle frame. They have received competing views from staff, students and parents.

- Expel her and show that rules are there to be obeyed.
- Expel her and show that River Valley High is strong on drugs and doesn't have a drug problem.

- Go easy. It's just marijuana; it's not cocaine or heroin or LSD, and it's pure, not refined. It wasn't intended to be smoked, and she wasn't dealing or supplying. It's no big deal.
- If we show compassion, how do we also show we're strong on illegal drugs?
- If we show compassion and appear weak on illegal drugs at the school, are we meeting our responsibility for the wellbeing of the other students in the school? We have a duty of care to all students.

They acknowledge these points and move to the temple/cathedral frame. They understand that there's a symbolic nature to this, and symbols, rituals, stories, music, ceremonies, and expressions of faith are all part of it, touching the heart as much as the head. This cuts through to why we're here. The discussion moves there now, and the team affirm that they believe they are leading with moral purpose in this decision. Questions follow:

- What are the main messages people will take from our decision? They need to be coherent.
- What is our narrative here? We have to take into account how our decision will be seen by the students, the staff, the parents and caregivers, and the wider community.
- We need to touch hearts as well as heads.
- How will we convey our decision, and to whom?

The team pause and check if they're confident they have covered the territory in depth. Have they missed anything? They agree that to the best of their ability they've stretched out on all four metaphors and they think they've got it covered as best they can. Now they'll sleep on it.

*

It's morning, and the team are back, ready to resume their deliberations. One of the deputy principals explains that she went to bed hoping she'd wake up with some way to simplify the complexity and show the way more clearly. She's woken this morning not with a silver bullet awaiting her, but with a passage from *Zorba the Greek* offering itself quietly in her mind, inviting her attention. It's been several years since she read it, but she's found the novel on her bookshelf this morning and brought it with her. She senses that there's something here for them. She says she's not sure why those words were there waiting for her this morning, but she suggests that the family and temple metaphors have been at work in her tortoise mind while she slept. She asks a little tentatively if she can read it to the group. With their encouragement, she reads.

> I remembered one morning when I discovered a cocoon in the bark of a tree, just as the butterfly was making a hole in its case and preparing to come out. I waited a while, but it was too long appearing and I was impatient. I bent over it and breathed on it to warm it. I warmed it as quickly as I could and the miracle began to happen before my eyes, faster than life. The case opened, the butterfly started slowly crawling out and I shall never forget my horror when I saw how its wings were folded back and crumpled; the wretched butterfly tried with its whole trembling body to unfold them. Bending over it, I tried to help it with my breath. In vain. It needed to be hatched out patiently and the unfolding of the wings should be a gradual process in the sun. Now it was too late. My breath had forced the butterfly to appear, all crumpled, before its time. It struggled desperately and, a few seconds later, died in the palm of my hand.
>
> That little body is, I do believe, the greatest weight I have on my conscience. For I realise today that it is a mortal sin to violate the great laws of nature. We should not hurry, we should not be impatient, but we should confidently obey the eternal rhythm.
>
> I sat on a rock to absorb this New Year's thought. Ah, if only that little butterfly could always flutter before me to show me the way. (Kazantzakis, 1959, pp. 132-33)

There's momentary silence, then the counsellor says she thinks she can see why those words found their way to the surface. "It's about Emily and us," she says. "I think it's a reminder to us about why we're really here, and a warning that there's danger: we could do damage if we rush things and get it wrong."

After a pause to think about that, Emily's English teacher says that it's strange, but she too woke with something from a novel hovering in her mind. She'd begun reading Frank Herbert's *Dune*, just a night or so ago. The opening sentence has stayed with her and she reads it out:

> A beginning is the time for taking the most delicate care that the balances are correct.

Again there's momentary quiet. The principal suggests that there's wisdom for them in those two excerpts: "I can see *dannelse* in there, reminding us that Emily isn't an adult; she's still becoming the Emily she's going to be.

And I can see danger as we take the first step in our decision because it's complicated and we need to get the balances right. So let's take that on board and go with the family and temple frames for a while and see where it takes us. Then we'll see if we've covered the others."

The other deputy takes them back to a statement they made earlier when stretching out on the family metaphor: "We often say that we see mistakes as learning opportunities, so how do we keep faith with that in this situation?" He goes on, "I think we agree that she needs to learn from this and also face some consequences. Can we achieve that without being overly punitive and squashing her feisty attitude? And without seeming to be soft on drugs? I think those are our 'delicate balances' from *Dune*."

The conversation becomes focused on that question, and further questions begin to morph into tentative answers. An hour later, the group feel they have exhausted those two frames and have decided on their first action. Emily is already at homeworking on this. They took that decision when they sent her home. During that time she is researching the state's laws and regulations about possession of illegal substances. She is doing a piece of writing to show she knows and understands those laws and regulations and how they apply to her actions in placing the marijuana leaf on the cover of her assignment and submitting it at school. She will be invited to return to school on Monday morning, where she and her mother will sit down with the leadership team and her home teacher to discuss Emily's findings. Assuming that goes well, she will return to class. The principal contacts Emily's mother and she is supportive of handling it in this way, assuring him she'll check in and make sure Emily completes the task successfully.

The temple frame is still challenging the team: What messages do they want to convey in their communication about the decision? Conversation ensues, and feeling confident they are making progress, they move on with two more questions:

- Have we drawn out all the possibilities from the four frames?
- How do we communicate the decision so we get the "delicate balances" right in what we want the decision to do?

They agree that in sending Emily home for the rest of the week the factory metaphor is adequately covered. The school will carry on as usual, and Emily's situation will be talked about, but the normal school routines won't be disrupted. The school and the wider community can see that the school's drugs policy is being enacted.

The family frame: They're showing care for Emily and duty of care for the other students.

The jungle: There will be some disagreement, but they will rely on the trust in their integrity and professionalism that they've worked on over the years.

They agree that the temple now needs completion through how they communicate the decision.

They agree they can't do any more without delaying communicating and implementing the decision.

We stay with the team now as they move to the final step: the communication of their decision.

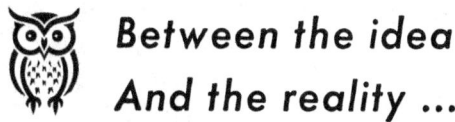
*Between the idea
And the reality ...*

- *What do you think about the progress the team have made? Are they getting it right?*
- *What do you think is their next big decision?*

CHAPTER 24

The power of story

> "Of the thousands of books published on the subject of leadership, only a few have hinted at the connection between leadership and storytelling." – Stephen Denning

> "A story is about significant events and memorable moments, not about time passing ... This is how the remembering self works: it composes stories and keeps them for future reference."
> – Daniel Kahneman

What is their story?

In 1839 the Spanish slave ship *La Amistad* was carrying a group of African men to Cuba to be sold as slaves in America. The Africans overwhelmed the captain and crew and took over the ship. In trying to sail back to Africa they were intercepted by an American naval ship and taken to Connecticut, where in January 1840 they were being tried in the United States Supreme Court for piracy and murder.

Theodore Joadson was an attorney defending the case for the Africans, but it was not going well. Joadson approached John Quincy Adams, ex-President of the United States, a lawyer and a strong anti-slavery advocate, asking his advice on how they might be able to turn things around to persuade the jury about the Africans' case.

The conversation is captured in the 1997 movie *Amistad*. According to the writer of the screenplay, David Franzoni, historically the following dialogue from the film captures the essence of what was said when Joadson met with Adams:

Adams: When I was an attorney, a long time ago, young man, I realised after much trial and error, that in a courtroom, whoever tells the best story wins. In unlawyer-like fashion, I give you that scrap of wisdom free of charge.

Joadson (Goes to leave): I'm much obliged for your time, sir.

Adams: What **is** their story, by the way?

Joadson: Sir?

Adams: What is their story?

Joadson: Why, they're, um ... from West Africa.

Adams: No. What is their **story**? Mr Joadson, you're from where originally?

Joadson: Why, Georgia, sir.

Adams: Georgia.

Joadson: Yes, sir.

Adams: Does that sum up who you are? A Georgian? Is that your story? No. You're an ex-slave, who's devoted his life to the abolition of slavery, and overcoming great hardships along the way, I should imagine. That's your story, isn't it? You and this young so-called lawyer have proven you know what they are. They're Africans. Congratulations. What you don't know, and haven't bothered in the least to discover, is who they are. (Screenplay from *Amistad*, 1997)

That conversation became the turning point in the case. The Africans' legal team went on to present the story of the captured Africans as fellow human beings, with homes and families, unlawfully deprived of their liberty and taken by force from their homeland. They had killed the captain and three crewmen of *La Amistad* in defence of their freedom, which was their right.

The jury ultimately accepted this story over that of the prosecution's story of the slaves as property to be bought and sold. John Quincy Adams was proven right: "In a courtroom, whoever tells the best story wins." So – does that also apply to a decision made in a school?

*

The River Valley leadership team had watched that scene from *Amistad* some years before with a leadership consultant, and had discussed and affirmed the power of story in presenting the case for an initiative they wanted to introduce. They stored it in the back-pack of their growing understanding about the management of meaning. They had agreed that with a decision made on a complex issue they would need to have an answer to John Quincy Adams's question to Theodore Joadson: *What is their story?* They decide this is the time to call on that wisdom as they turn to how they will handle the jungle and temple frames in communicating their decision. It's now their turn to decide what their story is.

"Which is to be master?"

You'll recall the conversation between Alice and Humpty Dumpty in Chapter 5. Alice questions whether words can mean many different things, as Humpty claims they can. His response, "The question is, which is to be master, that's all", is surely an example of the management of meaning. There are differing ways a situation can be presented, and the words used to communicate it are the key to carrying the message you want to convey. That is the challenge facing the River Valley leadership team. They have made their decision; now how do they communicate it in order to satisfy the diverse views in the school community about how Emily's situation should be handled?

They make a crucial, double-barrelled assumption: firstly, though some are calling for Emily to be expelled, the team are confident that very few people in the school or wider community wish her harm; secondly, everybody in the school or wider community believes she has to face consequences. There lies the common ground for communicating their decision. Their challenge is to grasp that this is the time for "taking the most delicate care that the balances are correct". Sensing that "balance" is going to be a key factor in their communication, they remind themselves that the school's motto is "In balance we grow". They can bring this decision back to the school's fundamental statement about why we are here.

*

Let's pause for a moment. Those words from *Dune* – "taking the most delicate care" – bring us back to Howard Gardner, and what he sees as the intimate relationship between leadership and story. Gardner offers a neatly nuanced claim:

> Leaders achieve their effectiveness chiefly through the stories they relate. Here, I use the term **relate** rather than **tell**, because presenting a story in words is but one way to communicate …

> The innovative leader takes a story that has been latent in the population, or among the members of his or her chosen domain, and brings new attention or a fresh twist to that story. (Gardner, 1995, pp. 9–10)

That's a reminder to the team that there are varying ways to communicate, and the second paragraph takes us back to Denmark, where the nation's philosophy of education rests on a unique Danish cultural belief, reinforced by a folk tale from their most famous author. But can an old story also be a modern one for its own times? Gardner takes us again to J. Robert Oppenheimer, suggesting that his story to his colleagues working on the Manhattan Project was a modern day "elemental story of identity", with a moral purpose:

> We scientists and technicians are blessed with certain knowledge and skills. As patriots, we must work together effectively, and as selflessly as possible, in order to produce a weapon that can help the Allies win the war. (Gardner, 1995, p. 97)

Drawing from Gardner, the team discuss various archetypal themes in stories and see some resonance with one, a theme that occurs in the stories of many cultures: a person makes a mistake, faces the consequences, is then given the opportunity to atone for the mistake, and goes on to contribute significant good for an individual, a family, or the tribe, village or other social entity. Two of Charles Dickens's characters come to mind: Sidney Carton in *A Tale of Two Cities*, who, after a drunken wasteful past, gives his life for his friend; and the escaped convict Magwitch in *Great Expectations*, who secretly contributes to the financial wellbeing of a young boy who cared for him when he was on the run. The Biblical story of the prodigal son is another example. Despite the poor behaviour of his son, the father never loses confidence in the boy's potential and his ability to learn from his mistakes and make good.

The team agree that while Emily's case is not as dramatic as those stories, the potential is there to tap that theme as a deeper layer in their communication without directly referring to it. If the meeting with Emily when she returns from suspension on Monday goes well, that will be the basis of the communication.

It does go well. Emily and her mother meet with the leadership team, and Emily has done well on the research about the legal implications of bringing that marijuana leaf to school. She shows clear understanding of the difficulty it placed the school in, and offers an emotional apology. The principal asks for her assurance that she won't try to get kudos from the other students for her actions, and she gives that assurance. He tells Emily that as far as the school authorities are concerned, as long as she keeps to that it's now closed and in the past. The team express their confidence in her as one of the student leaders in the school, and Emily sheds a tear as she heads off to join the other students in her next class.

The principal thanks Emily's mother for the way she has helped them to see the situation through, then the team have a quick conversation to affirm that they believe Emily is sincere in what she has said, and their confidence that she will go forward from here. They also gain confidence from the way Emily's mother has been so supportive and balanced throughout.

Now for the communication.

Less is more

The process has so far taken four school days, with the weekend in between. That afternoon, the leadership team reconvene to decide how they will communicate their decision.

The same deputy principal who brought the excerpt from *Zorba the Greek* is an admirer of Ernest Hemingway's writing, and she suggests they need to communicate their decision in plain words. She mentions Hemingway's ability to write simply but to imply feelings and emotion beneath the words so his words on the page actually have a stronger impact on the reader than if the emotions were stated overtly. The team agree that they will try to achieve this in the words they choose in communicating the decision; to convey sincerity and avoid the jargon that annoys so many people outside (and inside) education.

The principal picks up on this theme. He offers an analogy from music, explaining how the jazz musicians Miles Davis and Count Basie offered similar explanations to Hemingway about how they approached their playing. It was summed up by Basie – "What you leave out is as important as what you play" – and by Davis, who in his autobiography recalls the (then) young pianist in his band, Herbie Hancock, who was expressing frustration that there were places in Davis's music where he didn't know what to play. Davis's response:

> Then Herbie, don't play nothing if you don't know what to play. You know, just let it go; you don't have to be playing all the time ... Don't just play because you have eighty-eight keys to play. (Davis, 1989, p. 265)

A particular observation about Count Basie by a fellow jazz musician takes this further:

> My favourite band is Count Basie's all the way. He is direct. He keeps it simple and sincere, and swings at all times. (Eli Robinson in Dance, 1980, p. 5)

Eli Robinson says Basie's piano playing is "direct", "simple", and "sincere". If we apply those principles to communication beyond music, we have a likely recipe for success. When Robinson adds "and swings at all times", he is referencing the jazz musicians' code for people tapping their feet and moving to the music: it's about connecting with the listeners. Add that to the recipe and apply it to communication and it moves from a likely recipe to a powerful brew. That's what the principal is getting at. One of the deputies picks up on this and remembers an example from one of America's most successful communicators, four-times-elected President Franklin Roosevelt, who surely understood it too when he offered advice to his son about getting a message across when speaking in public: "Be brief; be sincere; be seated" (*Washington Post*, January 1940).

The team agree that they should avoid over-complicating their decision – despite the fact that it is complicated. Instead, they need to ensure that their communication comes through as sincere, not self-righteous with binary moralising about good and bad; simple but not simplistic – a quiet, calm communication that brings the school community together in a spirit of optimism and trust in the potential of young people, including Emily, and also carrying the message that River Valley High is strong on drugs. The conversation that follows evolves into a strategy essentially drawn from Ernest Hemingway, Count Basie and Miles Davis: *less is more*. They decide what they will do, and what they will leave out:

- Their message will be that Emily made a mistake; she understands that, she's atoned for it, and now she's going forward. They will express their confidence in Emily as a person and state their understanding that in placing an unrefined marijuana leaf on her assignment Emily had no intention of using, dealing or supplying an illegal substance to other students. At the same time, it wasn't a smart thing to do, and she has

faced the consequences. The school's drug policy remains strong and unchanged.
- They won't communicate their decision in writing, except for a brief notice on the staff-room notice-board explaining that Emily was suspended for three days, successfully completed a second research piece, and has returned to school. It's now in the past, and everyone is going forward. They will communicate this more fully and invite discussion at a staff meeting later in the week.
- The principal won't speak about it at Friday morning's assembly and there will be nothing in the school's weekly newsletter, because it would give the incident unwanted publicity and perhaps unintentionally publicly shame Emily.
- They will target influential groups in the school community and take them into their confidence, relating accurately but briefly what has happened, how they have handled it with Emily, and why they have handled it in this way. The principal will explain it to the School Board, which has parent and teacher representation, at a meeting later in the week. He will also explain it to the Parents and Friends Executive Committee at their monthly meeting next week; the deputy principals will explain it to the parent sub-committees they have responsibility for; and the leadership team will sit down with the Student Representative Council and explain it in similar fashion to the way they explained it for the adults. They will invite discussion at all those meetings.

They know they will be relying on the bed of trust and respect they have worked to establish in their relationships with the students, staff and parents/caregivers, hopeful their decision will rest on this in people's minds when the decision is communicated.

The leadership team's strategy is based on the assumption that anyone – adult or student or person from the wider community – who wants to ask about the incident and how it has been handled has access to many sources via the school's structures, all of which have received the same briefing. And those structures – Sergiovanni's systemsworld and represented in Bolman and Deal's factory frame – are resting on the culture of the school – its lifeworld: the vehicle for acting out the values, beliefs and norms. That's what guided their decision. They feel they have good reason to be quietly confident, as they have answered the questions posed by both John Quincy

Adams and Peggy Noonan to the best of their ability; and they have taken less than a week to reach the decision.

In case you're wondering – in her original essay to which she'd attached the marijuana leaf, Emily had argued against the legalisation of marijuana.

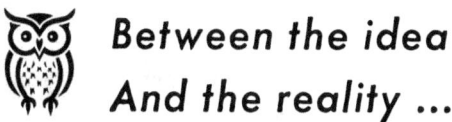
Between the idea
And the reality ...

Back in Chapter 8, I listed previous mistakes from my own experience, and it's timely to check back on those.

- *Have the River Valley team taken the time to enable their tortoise minds to balance their hare brains?*
- *Have they done the preparation to meet Abraham Lincoln's and Albert Einstein's problem-solving formulae in Chapter 7?*
- *Have they missed something, or have they seen everything but missed the importance of something? Have they given something more importance than is warranted?*
- *Have they seen the nuances that the age of ambiguity throws up every time they make a decision? Have they balanced intuition with intellect and emotion, and have they avoided the ever-present "noise"?*
- *Have they succeeded in making it simple, but not simplistic?*
- *What do you think of their communication process?*

How well have they done? You be the judge.

CHAPTER 25
Where it all leads

"Nobody else's wheel will work on your wagon." – Tom Sergiovanni

The metaphor for this journey we've taken together – *the long and winding road* – began in Chapter 3, and it's woven its way through to here. You've probably identified its source as a Beatles' song from 1970. When you read those words in Chapter 3, I wonder if you took in the complete line from the song. In case you didn't, here it is again:

The long and winding road, that leads to your door ...

And there lies the most important theme that has influenced my thinking about educational leadership and decision-making, and the most important learning I wanted to share with you. That's because, to quote another line from the song:

I've seen that road before ...

Based on my experience, my intuition, my reading, and my formal and informal study over the years, my deepest message to you is this: it all leads to your door. You can't outsource or avoid your leadership. There is no blueprint or formula for decision-making; but there is wisdom, there is the management of meaning, and there are your mindscapes. The River Valley team had a leadership framework to guide them in reaffirming *why we are here*. They also had a framework for analysing the problem – Bolman and Deal's reframing process – but that didn't solve the problem for them; it helped them to be confident they'd covered all the angles while being true to themselves; and they understood that ultimately it would lead to their door.

I've learnt that to be the authentic and effective educational leader you want to be, you have to do the thinking. By all means do it collaboratively, base it on research and a credible framework, bring your values and beliefs to it, your intuition, as you must, and importantly, sleep on it. Then have the confidence to come to a decision. Despite books that offer *5 easy steps to effective decision-making* or *Decision-making made easy*, there's no universal formula, and there's no way to make it easy. Every context is different, and that's why you have to engage in the management of meaning in your own context: to analyse and synthesise the situation, reflect on it, and tell the story of your decision. And Simon Sinek was right: it always comes back to "why". Tom Sergiovanni understood this over 30 years ago:

> You have to reinvent the wheel whether you want to or not, because nobody else's wheel will work on your wagon. (Sergiovanni, 1992, p. 115)

Like that quote, the concepts are simple, but working through them and ultimately acting on them is not. It's difficult, nuanced territory. I've invited you to walk the road with me through that territory, exploring the uneasy mix of congruence, ambivalence and tension that is always there, leading to your door. It's over to you. I hope you've found it challenging, affirming and uplifting.

Above all, I hope that having accepted the invitation to walk with me on this journey, you'll find yourself wiser, both as a person and as a leader; that your work will be more meaningful to you than it was before you read this book; and that it will give you some peace of mind as you continue to make decisions in the most challenging of roles: that of an educational leader in the age of ambiguity.

Afterword

"I write entirely to find out what I'm thinking, what I'm looking at, what I see and what it means. What I want and what I fear."
– Joan Didion

"I write to find what it is in my head that's trying to get out."
– John Steinbeck

This book has rolled around in my head for 10 years or so, at times annoying me in the extreme as it's refused to go away. Finally, I heeded Joan Didion and John Steinbeck and started to write, not knowing what would flow, if anything. Something did, and you're holding it in your hand.

I knew it would be about leadership, but once I started writing, what was in my head trying to get out started to reveal itself. "What I'm thinking" soon turned out to be about decision-making, and as I wrote, "what I see", "what I'm looking at" and "what it means" gradually took form. As for "what I fear": I think that emerged as the concern that younger educators coming into school leadership might be seduced by the charismatic, decisive, action-oriented model of leadership and decision-making which still has significant traction despite being questioned and challenged over many decades of research (and in my own experience and observations). Indeed, Alexander Pope knew it in 1711 when he wrote:

> Fools rush in where angels fear to tread.

*

Emily is not her real name, but the marijuana leaf incident is based on a real event that my leadership team and I and other teachers addressed at Hillbrook some years ago. It taxed our leadership capabilities further than we'd had to go before, occurring at a time when the city and the area in which the school is located were experiencing a significant issue with drug use by young people, including some recent deaths by overdose from street drugs in the wider community. Added to that, Queensland law included marijuana in the same classification as all illegal drugs, and the laws were strongly policed. Parents were particularly nervous about it and teachers and school leaders were often asked variations on the question, "What are you doing about drugs?" As principal, the school's duty of care rested with me, and we had to get it right.

To the best of my recollection, the decision-making process and our professional learning preceding it evolved in much the way I've described here, with some minor elaboration or omissions in the interest of clarity. Some of our thinking drew indirectly from our experience, our personal reading, professional learning and research, and was perhaps not as overt as I've implied here. I'm confident, though, that we drew from the sources I've indicated, and that the process we followed and the flow of the process are essentially accurate. I've tried to simplify it without being simplistic.

*

I've researched widely and drawn from many sources, but there are a few people whose writing and thinking have played an important role in my thinking over the years, and they have influenced the writing of this book: Frank Crowther, Emeritus Professor, University of Southern Queensland; Thomas Sergiovanni, Lillian Professor of Education and Administration, and founder of the Trinity Principals' Centre San Antonio; Peter Senge, Sloan School, Massachusetts Institute of Technology; Daniel Kahneman, Emeritus Professor of Psychology and Public Affairs, Princeton University; and Guy Claxton, University of Bristol.

I highly commend their writing and thinking to all educational leaders: they have much to offer, well beyond what I've cited in this book.

References

Agassi, A. (2009). *Open*. Harper Collins.
Albrechtsen, J. (2023, December 13). My truth? What about the truth? From halls of learning to an intellectual wasteland. *The Australian*.
Alvy, H., & Robbins, P. (2010). *Learning from Lincoln*. ASCD.
Angelou, M. (2004, July 27). *Address to Democratic National Convention*, Boston.
Argyris, C. (2000). *Flawed advice & the management trap*. Oxford University Press.
Argyris, C. & Schön, D. (1996). *Organisational learning II*. Addison-Wesley.
Barrett, F. J. (2012). *Yes to the mess*. Harvard Business Review Press.
Barth, R. (1990). *Improving schools from within*. Jossey-Bass.
Bate, J., & Rasmussen, E. (Eds.) (2007). *William Shakespeare: Complete works*. Royal Shakespeare Company, The Modern Library.
Beare, H. (1987). *Teach hope*. Presentation to Australian College of Education National Conference, Sydney.
Beckett, S. (1955). *Waiting for Godot*. Reclam Universal Bibliothek.
Bird, K., & Sherwin, M. J. (2005). *American Prometheus: The triumph & tragedy of J. Robert Oppenheimer*. Atlantic Books.
Block, P. (2008). *Community*. Berrett-Koehler.
Blount, S., & Leinwand, P. (2019). Why are we here? *Harvard Business Review*, November–December 2019.
Bolman, L., & Deal, T. (2011). *Leading with soul*. Jossey-Bass.
Bolman, L., & Deal, T. (2013). *Reframing organisations* (5th Ed.). Jossey-Bass.
Browning, P. (2020). *Principled*. University of Queensland Press.
Bryk, A., & Schneider, B. (2002). *Trust in schools*. Russell Sage Foundation.
Burns, K. (1990). *The Civil War*. DVD. Magna Pacifica.
Carroll, J. (2023). *The saviour syndrome*. Sutherland House.
Carroll, L. (1998). *Alice's adventures in wonderland and through the looking-glass*. Penguin.
Clark, A. (2022). *Making Australian history*. Vintage Books.
Claxton, G. L. (1997). *Hare brain, tortoise mind: Why intelligence increases when you think less*. Fourth Estate.
Colvin, G. (2016). *Talent is overrated*. Nicholas Brealey.
Cosgrove, P. (2007). *My story*. Harper Collins.
Covey, S. M. R. (2018). *The speed of trust*. The Free Press.
Covey, S. R. (1992). *Principle-centred leadership*. Fireside.
Covey, S. R. (2000). *The 7 Habits of highly effective people*. The Business Library.

Covey, S. R., Merrill, A., & Merrill, R. (1994). *First things first*. Simon & Schuster.
Crowther, F., & Boyne, K. (2016). *Energising teaching*. ACER.
Crowther, F., Kaagan, S., Ferguson, M., & Hann, L. (2002). *Developing teacher leaders*. Corwin.
Crowther, F., with Fox, K., & Addison, B. (2021). *Inspiring hope*. Hawker Brownlow.
Dance, S. (1980). *The world of Count Basie*. Da Capo Press.
Davis, M. (1989). *Miles: The autobiography*. Simon & Schuster.
De Carvalho, D. (2024, January 20). Modern Western malaise 500 years in the making. *The Weekend Australian*.
Deal, T., & Peterson, K. (2016). *Shaping school culture*. Jossey-Bass.
Denning, S. (2004). *Squirrel Inc*. Jossey-Bass.
Deveson, I. (1997). *Evolution of an Australian management style*. Business & Professional Publishing.
Dickens, C. (2008). *Hard times*. Oxford University Press.
Dickenson, E. (1998). In A. Carroll, S. Iyengar, H. Labalme, D. Maclean, & E. Elam Roth (Eds.) *101 great American poems*. Dover Publications.
Didion, J. (1976, December 6). Why I write. *The New York Times*.
Dockrill, P. (2021). Facts are no longer convincing. *Science Alert*. https://www.sciencealert.com/facts-are-no-longer-convincing-research-suggests-you-should-say-this-instead
Drucker, P. F. (2006). *Classic Drucker*. Harvard Business Press.
Dweck, C. (2006). *Mindset*. Robinson.
Edmonds, M., & Duncan, R. (2018). *Truth, growth, respect*. Wiley.
Eliot, T. S. (1977). *The complete poems & plays of T. S. Eliot*. Redwood Burn.
Ergas, H. (2023, January 6). From the horrors of Hitler's war to a life devoted to truth. *The Australian*.
Evans, R. (1996). *The human side of school change*. Jossey-Bass.
Franzoni, D. (1997). *Amistad*. Screenplay. Dreamworks Pictures.
Fullan, M. (1999). *Change forces: The sequel*. Falmer Press.
Fullan, M. (2001). *Leading in a culture of change*. Jossey-Bass.
Fullan, M. (2020). *Leading in a culture of change* (2nd Ed.). Jossey-Bass.
Gardner, H. (1995). *Leading minds*. Basic Books.
Gladwell, M. (2005). *Blink*. Penguin.
Gladwell, M. (2009). *Outliers*. Penguin.
Gleick, J. (1988). *Chaos: The amazing science of the unpredictable*. Minerva.
Gleick, J. (1999). *Faster: The acceleration of just about everything*. Little, Brown.
Goldsmith, O. (1770). *The deserted village*. Kessinger Publishing.
Goleman, D. (2002). *Primal leadership*. Harvard Business School Press.
Goleman, D. (2006). *Working with emotional intelligence*. Bantam Books.
Goleman, D. (2014). *Focus*. Bloomsbury.
Goodwin, D. K. (2005). *Team of rivals*. Penguin.
Goodwin, D. K. (2018). *Leadership: Lessons from the presidents for turbulent times*. Viking.
Gordon, G. T. (2004). In A. Russo (Ed.), *School reform in Chicago*. Harvard Education Press.
Gorman, A. (2021). *Call us what we carry*. Penguin Random House.

Graham, D. (2023). Interview with the author in *Armi Nius*, July, PIB-NGIB-HQ-PIR Association, Brisbane, Australia.
Hagstrom, D. (2004). *From outrageous to inspired*. Jossey-Bass.
Hattie, J. (2009). *Visible learning*. Routledge.
Hattie, J., & Zierer, K. (2018). *10 mindframes for visible learning*. Routledge.
Havel, V. (1991). *Disturbing the peace*. Random House.
Hawkins, D. (Ed.). (1969). *D. H. Lawrence: Stories, essays & poems*. Dent.
Hemingway, E. (1959). *A moveable feast*. Panther.
Hentoff, N. (1985). *The jazz life*. Da Capo Press.
Herbert, F. (1966). *Dune*. Hodder & Stoughton.
Horowitz, A. (2013). *On looking*. Simon & Schuster.
Kahneman, D. (2011). *Thinking, fast and slow*. Penguin.
Kahneman, D., Sibony, O., & Sunstein, C. (2021). *Noise*. William Collins.
Kazantzakis, N. (1959). *Zorba the Greek*. Bruno Cassirer.
Kegan, R. (1994). *In over our heads*. Harvard University Press.
Keneally, T. (2008). *Abraham Lincoln: A life*. Penguin.
Kenny, C. (2023, November 4). Robust public debate is the best answer to spin. *The Weekend Australian*, p. 23.
Kochanek, J. (2005). *Building trust for schools*. Corwin.
Kubin, E., Puryear, C., Schein, C., & Gray, K. (2021). Personal experiences bridge moral and political divides better than facts. *Proceedings of the National Academy of Sciences, 118*(6).
Kuran, T., & Sunstein, C. (1999). Availability cascades and risk regulation. *Stanford Law Review, 51*(4).
Lennon, J., & McCartney, P. (1967). "Strawberry fields forever". Northern Songs.
Lerner, A. J., & Loewe, F. (1964). *My Fair Lady*. Warner Brothers Pictures.
Limerick, D., Cunnington, B., & Crowther, F. (1998). *Managing the new organisation (2nd Ed.)*. Business & Professional Publishing.
Lloyd, G. (2022, April 6). Grand climate narrative limits our solutions. *The Australian*.
MacBeath, J. (2004). *The leadership file*. Learning Files.
MacBeath, J., Frost, D., Swaffield, S., & Waterhouse, J. (2003). *Making the connections: The story of a seven country odyssey in search of a practical theory*. University of Cambridge, Faculty of Education.
Mackay, H. (1994). *Why don't people listen?* Pan MacMillan.
Mackay, H. (2010). *What makes us tick?* Hachette.
Macklin, R. (Ed.) (2006). *My favourite teacher*. University of New South Wales Press.
Mandela, N. (1997). *Long walk to freedom*. Abacus.
Marquet, D. (2015). *Turn the ship around*. Penguin.
Mathews, J. (1988). *Escalante*. Henry Holt.
McCartney, P. (1970). "The long & winding road". Apple Music.
McGuiness, M. (2004). *You've got personality*. MaryMac Books.
McMillen, A. (2022, October 22). The Collier Effect. *Weekend Australian Review*.
Miki, M. (2021). *Quietly powerful*. Major Street Publishing.
Moos, L., & MacBeath, J. (Eds.). (2004). *Democratic learning*. Routledge Falmer.
Morgan, G. (1986). *Images of organisation*. Sage Publications.
Muller, J. Z. (2018). *The tyranny of metrics*. Princeton University Press.
Murphy, J. (2019). *Incentivology*. Hardie Grant.

Murray, D. (2019). *The madness of crowds*. Bloomsbury.
Noonan, P. (1998). *Simply speaking*. Regan Books.
Noyes, A. (1906). *The highwayman*. Oxford Children's Classics, Oxford University Press.
Obama, M. (2018). *Becoming*. Penguin Random House.
Orwell, G. (1947). *1984*. Penguin.
Palmer, P. (2007). *The courage to teach* (10th anniversary edition). Jossey-Bass.
Peters, T. (1991). *Thriving on chaos*. Harper Collins.
Pink, D. (2022). *The power of regret*. Canongate Books.
Pope, A. (2014). *An essay on criticism*. Cambridge University Press.
Purtell, C. (2022). The new science of forgetting. *Time*, May 9/May 16.
Rodin, J. (2015). *The resilience dividend*. Profile Books.
Rogers, E. (2003). *Diffusion of innovations*. Free Press.
Rosenthal, R., & Jacobsen, L. (1992). *Pygmalion in the classroom* (new expanded edition). Random House.
Rosling, H., with Rosling, O., & Rosling Rönnlund, A. (2018). *Factfulness*. Sceptre.
Russo, A. (Ed.). (2004). *School reform in Chicago*. Harvard Education Press.
Sahlberg, P., & Walker, T. (2021). *In teachers we trust*. Norton.
Sartre, J.-P. (1945). *Les Temps Modernes*. First issue.
Sartre, J.-P. (1974). *Nausea*. Penguin.
Schlesinger, R. (2009). *White House ghosts*. Simon & Schuster.
Seeger, P. (1963). "Where have all the flowers gone?" Columbia Records.
Senge, P. (1992). *The fifth discipline*. Random House.
Senge, P. (Ed.). (2000). *Schools that learn*. Nicholas Brealey.
Sergiovanni, T. (1992). *Moral leadership*. Jossey-Bass.
Sergiovanni, T. (2000). *The lifeworld of leadership*. Jossey-Bass.
Shaw, G. B. (1946). *The complete plays of Bernard Shaw*. Colorgravure.
Silver, N. (2012). *The signal and the noise*. Penguin.
Sinek, S. (2011). *Start with why*. Portfolio/Penguin.
Sinek, S. (2019). *The infinite game*. Penguin Business.
Stafford, W. (2017). In W. Sieghart (Ed.), *The poetry pharmacy*. Particular Books.
Steinbeck, E., & Wallsten, R. (Eds.). (1979). *Steinbeck: A life in letters*. Pan.
Surowiecki, J. (2004). *The wisdom of crowds*. Little, Brown.
Sutton, P. C. (1998). *Pieter de Hooch 1629-1684*. Yale University Press.
Toffler, A. (1970). *Future shock*. Random House.
Vaill, P. (1984). The purposing of high-performing systems. In T. Sergiovanni & J. Corbally (Eds.), *Leadership & organisational culture*. University of Illinois Press.
Weick, K. (1977). Educational organisations as loosely coupled systems. *Administrative Science Quarterly, 21*, 1-22.
Westover, T. (2018). *Educated*. Windmill Books.
Whitman, W. (1949). *Leaves of grass*. Holt, Rhinehart & Winston.
Williams, B. R. (1970). A. P. Elkin - Grand old man of Australian anthropology. *University of Sydney News, 2*(6), 2.
Yeats, W. B. (1990). *Collected poems*. Picador.

www.ingramcontent.com/pod-product-compliance
Lightning Source LLC
Chambersburg PA
CBHW050354120526
44590CB00015B/1690